# MOMMY LIED TO GOD

There is
Story in Your
Story.

# "Mommy Lied to God"

## LIFE LESSONS IN AUTHENTIC STORYTELLING

### CARLOS MAESTAS

*Carlos Maestas*

geekdom media

MOMMY LIED TO GOD

*Life Lessons in Authentic Storytelling*

ISBN  978-1-5445-0402-5 *Paperback*

978-1-5445-0403-2 *Ebook*

*Illustrations by Rick Lopez.*

*To the co-founders of my story,*
*my mom and dad.*

# Contents

# Introduction

Anyone who grew up between 1968 and 2001 no doubt experienced one of the greatest storytellers America has ever produced. Maybe *the* best. You might think I mean Walt Disney. His resume is undeniable: the creator of Mickey Mouse, Cinderella, Snow White. Disneyland and, later, Walt Disney World. Winner of twenty-two Oscars.

I understand, but you would be wrong. I say this at risk of being added to the Disney corporation's version of the TSA no-fly list. As I write this, I am having real anxiety about the next time I drive my family halfway across the country like Clark Griswold, only to have my Magic Band confiscated at the gate. "Mommy, why does Mickey Mouse hate Daddy?"

Don't get me wrong, I love everything Disney, but for me, Fred Rogers of *Mr. Rogers' Neighborhood* fame, is one of the greatest storytellers in American history, and probably the most iconic children's storyteller *ever*. I reflected on his legacy recently as I flew to New York City and watched the documentary *Won't You Be My Neighbor?* The film is a heartwarming look at the life of the legendary children's television pioneer.

For three decades, Fred came into our homes to educate, entertain, and inspire a generation of kids, and his show was a masterclass on the power of authentic storytelling. Storytelling is one of the most powerful tools we have to reach our fullest potential in life, and Mr. Rogers embodies the kind of storytelling at the heart of this book. Here are the three main reasons why.

## I. HE TACKLED REAL ISSUES

Walt Disney created a captivating lineup of unforgettable characters, but none of their storylines dealt with divorce, racism, or the threat of impending nuclear war. It is hard to imagine Prince Charming complaining about paying child support or Aladdin using a wish to stop all the gentrification in Agrabah.[1] Mr. Rogers, though, believed that kids could understand difficult issues presented honestly and in an age-appropriate way.

Rogers also incorporated his deep religious faith in his

---

1    I hear it's become a real problem. I am sure Starbucks is to blame, somehow.

storytelling. Before finding his calling on public television, he obtained a Master in Divinity and became an ordained Presbyterian minister. It is not hard to see how his television show would become his ministry. After Dr. Martin Luther King, Jr.'s assassination, he devoted an entire episode of the show to answering children's questions about the slain civil rights leader's tragic death.

He fought racism by introducing the first recurring part for an African American on a children's show when he cast Francois Clemmons as "Officer Clemmons." In one amazing segment, the two soaked their feet in a shared wading pool. Mr. Rogers later dried Officer Clemmons's feet with a towel. It was a bold move, and it is hard to overstate the importance of foot washing as an act of humility and a symbol of reverence straight out of the Bible.

Other times, Mr. Rogers tackled issues like childhood disease and disability. Jeffrey Erlanger was a ten-year-old boy confined to a wheelchair as the result of a spinal tumor. Seeing a quadriplegic child would spark questions in any youngster. In one of his most famous episodes, Mr. Rogers welcomed Jeffrey to the show, had him explain his condition and show off his chair. More importantly, he gave Jeffrey a chance to show that what he lacked in mobility he made up for in personality and spirit.

The stories Mr. Rogers shared were the opposite of the

Disney fairy tale. They were real and handled with honesty—a lesson you'll learn to apply to your own storytelling as we move through this book. Together, like Mr. Rogers would have wanted his neighbors to do.


## 2. HE WAS AUTHENTIC

During the documentary, director Morgan Neville makes one thing clear: Mr. Rogers was the same guy on and off the screen. Early in his career, Mr. Rogers made it a point to just be himself no matter whether the cameras were rolling.

"One of the greatest gifts you can give anybody," he once said, "is the gift of your honest self. I believe kids can spot a phony a mile away." He did not try to be something that he was not. He looked completely comfortable in his cardigan, tie, and sneakers. His show ran for over three decades, yet he made no attempt to try to keep up with the latest look. He never traded in his sweater for a leather jacket or his low-top sneakers for a pair of basketball shoes. (Okay, it might have been cool to see Mr. Rogers rocking some Jordans, but it simply was not him.) Mr. Rogers was not interested in making a fashion statement. What he was interested in was giving generations of children a sense of security through the predictable practice of changing from his sports coat to his sweater and sneakers. Brilliant! It was so impactful, in fact, the practice continues to this day through the animated spin-off of Mr. Rogers's show, *Daniel Tiger's Neighborhood*.

Mr. Rogers was not just consistent when it came to his choice of dress.

There is a wonderful firsthand account of an encounter with Rogers by journalist and novelist, Anthony Breznican, following a global tragedy.

In May 2017, a suicide bomber in Manchester, England detonated a suicide bomb outside an Ariana Grande concert. Twenty people lost their lives. In the days that followed, many people posted a famous quote from Mr. Rogers on social media: "When I was a boy and I would see scary things in the news, my mother would say to me, 'Look for the helpers. You will always find people who are helping.'"

Breznican added a story of another Rogers encounter he had when he was in college and in need of help. He tweeted about a dark season in his life. He felt lonely and hopeless, and he struggled to find some inspiration. One day, he stumbled upon an episode playing in the common area of his dorm building. As he sat and watched an entire episode, the calming, familiar voice of his favorite neighbor instantly made him feel better.

A few days later, he entered an elevator and locked eyes with Mr. Rogers, who greeted him with a warm smile. He tried to play it cool. It worked for a minute, but before he walked out of the elevator, he turned to Mr. Rogers and said,

"Mr. Rogers, I don't mean to bother you, but I wanted to say thanks."

Mr. Rogers smiled and asked, "Did you grow up as one of my neighbors?"

Breznican fought back tears as he replied yes.

Mr. Rogers opened up his arms for a hug, and said, "It's great to see you again, neighbor."

Before Breznican knew it, he was pouring out his heart to Mr. Rogers, telling him about rediscovering the show when he most needed it. Then, Mr. Rogers took off his scarf and motioned to a window ledge. He sat down and said, "Do you want to tell me what was upsetting you?"

Breznican had just lost his grandfather a few months before and was struggling to mourn without family or close friends to confide in. Mr. Rogers had been the first person to ask, "What is upsetting you?" Mr. Rogers went on to share about the loss of his own grandfather and said, "You'll never stop missing the people. You'll always carry with you what they taught you and how they shaped you as a person."

Breznican later wrote that when Mr. Rogers passed away in 2003, it deeply touched him: "I wasn't crying over the death of a celebrity. I was mourning the loss of a neighbor."

As Rogers showed with his interaction with Breznican, his on-camera persona of a calm and kind educator who loved his audience worked because it was authentic. Were any of you naughty neighbors expecting Mr. Rogers to have a dark side? By all accounts it simply did not exist.[2] Rogers taught us all a valuable lesson in authenticity: give the gift of your honest self. You'll learn to apply this principle to your storytelling as we move through this book. Again, together—the Mr. Rogers way.

## 3. HIS STORIES MOVED PEOPLE

Another distinguishing characteristic differentiating Disney and Mr. Rogers was the money at their disposal. During his peak years, Disney had vast sums available to bring his vision to life, while Mr. Rogers had only a small budget to communicate to his audience.

He had no army of animators.

No big studio backing him.

What he did have, though, was a ragtag team, his puppets, and his own voice. And that was enough. He was head writer, composer, producer, showrunner, and host, all rolled in

---

2   There is a meme floating around with Mr. Rogers flipping kids the bird. That was just Mr. Rogers keeping it real. Sometimes crazy stuff can go down when you are singing "Where Is Thumbkin," and you get to Tall-Man. Also, how many parents among us have not at least desired to shoot our kids the finger at some point?

one. He understood that if he created meaningful content aimed at the heart, he would build trust with the kids who depended on him. As he proved over the next three decades, his instincts were perfect.

Mr. Rogers did not just connect with children. His gift for simplifying his story quite literally saved the network on which his show appeared. In 1969, the administration of President Nixon slashed the Public Broadcasting Service (PBS) budget. The network needed $20 million at the time to save itself (equivalent to about $140 million in today's dollars).

Two days of Congressional testimony on PBS's behalf left the network on the cusp of extinction. Its future hung by a frayed string. Senator John Pastore of Rhode Island chaired the committee and seemed to be the man who held the fate of PBS in his hands. He portrayed himself as a tough guy, ripped from the pages of a Mario Puzo screenplay. When Mr. Rogers came before him to testify, it paralleled the scene from *The Godfather* where Amerigo Bonasera meets with Don Vito Corleone in a darkened office to ask for a favor on the day of his daughter's wedding.[3]

Instead of adhering to his prepared statement, Mr. Rogers took seven minutes and told a story. He didn't have Pow-

---

3  According to the movie, no Sicilian is supposed to refuse a request on the day of his daughter's wedding.

erPoint, props, or bar graphs. He spoke with conviction, confidence, and clarity. He explained his show's mission: to make each child feel authentically made and special just for being exactly who they were. He showcased the value of his product by persuading the audience—Pastore and his colleagues—to reflect on their own kids and their own childhood. He drew a clear distinction between what he offered and the animated cartoons then dominating kids' television, which portrayed violence as funny.

His show, he said, had a budget of $6,000, which paid for thirty minutes of programming, versus two minutes of cartoons.

He ended his story with the lyrics to a song: "What do you do with the mad that you feel? When you feel so mad you could bite? When the whole wide world seems oh so wrong and nothing you do seems very right? It's great to be able to stop when you plan the thing that's wrong, and be able to do something instead and think about this song." Such a beautiful lesson, delivered in an alternative way, to teach a child how to deal with anger.

By the end of the speech, Sen. Pastore made it clear that PBS would get its money. Why? Mr. Rogers had moved people— exactly what you'll learn to do as we journey together in the following pages.

Again—you guessed it neighbors—together.

## COOL, BUT I AM NO MR. ROGERS

Throughout history, storytelling has been a conduit for the power to transform a message into a movement. Maybe you don't consider yourself among the movement makers, but there are still pivotal moments in all our lives when we need to share our story to achieve a goal. We are all storytellers. We share our story when we apply for jobs, seek scholarships, or convince someone we're worthy of a second date.[4]

For professionals, opportunities for storytelling are everywhere. Consider the entrepreneur explaining her startup to a room of potential investors. Or the pastor at a hipster church who needs to capture the attention of a congregation of multitasking millennials.

Storytelling is not some perk or something "good to have." It can mean the difference between success and failure. It can mean the difference between finding your "why" and finding yourself wandering aimlessly.

Meaningful storytelling is the secret ingredient that turns mere facts into meaningful connections.

I've made a career of finding and promoting those connections for almost two decades. I have led nonprofits and businesses of all sizes through storytelling workshops. I have had the terrifying responsibility of guiding middle-

---

4   If you suggest to split the bill, no amount of storytelling is going to help.

and high school-aged students through biblical messages as a youth pastor. I have worked to make ancient biblical principles relatable and to connect emotionally while teaching weekend services for a 1,400 member church. Years of performance as a standup comic showed me how to simplify the message and elicit an emotional response. My lab was the hundreds of performances in comedy clubs, universities, theaters, dive bars, nightclubs, class reunions, Narcotics Anonymous meetings, and corporate holiday parties. My jokes are funnier when people are drinking, so feel free to pour your favorite beverage while you read this book if it helps.

Being able to tell your story can mean the difference between an idea that changes the world and one that dies on the vine. Nothing is more important than your story. It has power. It is what people will remember about you. It can bring purpose to your pain. It can differentiate you and connect you to an audience simultaneously.

Every audience expects to go on a journey with a clear destination. This book will help you meet that challenge by teaching you the characteristics of authentic storytelling. Your story has the power to influence emotion in any room, and when you can stir emotion, you have a great chance to inspire action. The goal of great storytelling isn't just getting people to understand what you want them to know, it is to make them feel something in the process.

Sketch Note Summary—Introduction

# CHAPTER ONE

# We All Have a Story

The first step to becoming a great storyteller is acknowledging that you have one. Margaret Atwood, author of *The Handmaid's Tale* said, "You're never going to kill storytelling, because it's built in the human plan. We come with it." Storytelling is in our DNA, and it is important to acknowledge that it happens with or without any effort from us. Our stories are shared by competitors, the media, and gossipy grandmas. When we don't intentionally participate in sharing our stories, we allow others to fill in the gaps. It is important to own all aspects of our story, whether they are good, bad, or ugly. I am not suggesting that you introduce yourself like, "Hi, my name is Bill. I am an accountant from Buffalo who has been divorced twice because I like to gamble." Storytelling requires some emotional intelligence, but when deployed correctly it can be the most powerful tool we have.

In this chapter we will discuss some common reasons we struggle to share our story and how we can start to develop a storytelling mindset.

## KEY IDEA: THERE IS GLORY IN OUR STORY

### MY STORY IS NOT WORTHY

Maybe you think your life is not that interesting. I get it. Your last name does not end in Kardashian, and no one is keeping up with you. Your social media following is better described as a quorum. Maybe your ideas don't always win because there are stronger personalities in the office. Despite all that, you must recognize that *you* already have the tools needed to become a great storyteller. Those tools are your life experiences and the experiences of those who came before you. Where you were born, what your parents did, that time you tried to be a male model but realized you are not very tall, the fact that you are medium height, have a lazy eye, and aren't that good-looking. Maybe that was just me.

If you have struggled to find strength in your story, I can relate. I was barely twenty-two when I started Key Ideas. I had no shortage of ambition back then, but I knew I lacked experience. I partnered with a husband-and-wife team that had been in the advertising business for twenty-five years.

Margaret had a kind way about her and would always greet you with a warm smile. She was the smartest person in the office but never let you feel intimidated. Years before I met her, she'd had a stroke while on board an airplane and almost died, and I am certain that that experience taught her the value of being fully present for the people she cared about.

Her husband John was the salesman. He's the kind of guy who has never been tall but enters a room like he is riding atop a float at the Macy's Thanksgiving Day parade. Once, I remember him showing up to a client meeting twenty minutes late. After being ushered in the room, he announced, "Gentlemen, I am back on schedule, so I will be twenty minutes late from now on." No apologies. Pure confidence. It was hard to see past all this, for a twenty-two-year-old kid who had even less life experience than John had work experience.

After a few months, a big contract that I had been working on fell through, and John decided to annul our partnership. He called me into his office and said he could no longer allow me to come to his building and "play business."[5] It was a punch in the gut and very well could have been the end of my story as an entrepreneur. Lucky for me, I had recently received another reality check that equipped me with an extra bit of motivation. The girl I had been dating

---

5  To this day, it is still one of the assholiest things someone has ever said to me, and I kind of respect him for it.

for only a few months announced that we were going to be having a baby. We got married later that year, and Elijah was born a month before Key Ideas' one-year anniversary. Elijah just turned seventeen. I still have Key Ideas. I don't still have that wife.

These are my stories. I own them. For better or worse, I have earned them. They are archived and ready to be tapped when I need to be reminded how far I have come. It would be easy to look at my failures and come to the conclusion that my story is not worthy. I now believe there is glory in my story.

Your experiences are what differentiate you, but they also have the power to help you connect with others. Think about your story like an electrical circuit. It takes both the positive and the negative to make a connection complete. If we choose to just focus on the positive, we run the risk of sounding inauthentic. If we choose to just focus on the negative, we also run the risk of a disconnection...and depressing a lot of people.

As I write this, there are over twenty democratic candidates vying to be president of the United States. Each of them is trying to convince America that their story is worthy of getting them elected to the most powerful position in the free land. Listen to any debate and hear how they insert their personal story into their list of accomplishments. Politicians can't get elected without connecting with their audience. It is a skill. It is something we can learn to do.

I had an opportunity to attend the formal announcement that Julian Castro, San Antonio Mayor and Housing and Urban Development Secretary, was running for president. As he stood in the same neighborhood on the west side of San Antonio that he grew up in, it was hard not to be moved. I think of my own kids, who at this moment in history can't look back and see a president that looks like them. I can't even think of a Hispanic actor that has played president on TV. The show *The West Wing* came close. They let Jimmy Smits get elected right before they canceled the show. We never got to see what he would do. The TV show *Scandal* elected a character played by San Antonio-native Ricardo Chavira just to have him assassinated as he was making his acceptance speech. Not cool, Shonda Rhimes. Let a brown brother lead the country for at least one season. It is like even Hollywood is afraid a Hispanic president is going to fill the white house with Virgin Mary candles and move his mom into a casita in the back.[6] Or maybe they are afraid he will get his cousins to renovate the White House and try to flip it. It's hard to know.

I guess what I am trying to say is, I was filled with pride as I

---

6  No doubt, when this finally happens, the secret service will gain at least twenty pounds. "Mr. President, your mom's tortillas have become a threat to our national security."

saw my city's former mayor stand in front of a huge crowd and say, "I am not a front-runner in this race, but I have not been a front-runner at anytime in my life. No one in the neighborhood I grew up in was ever a front-runner. When my grandmother got here almost one hundred years ago, I'm sure she never could have imagined that just two generations later, one of her grandsons would be serving as a member of the United States Congress and the other would be standing with you here today to say these words: I am a candidate for President of the United States of America." It was his moment, but through a carefully crafted story, it also belonged to anyone who's own family came to the country with a hope and a dream for a better future for the next generation.

Castro also said, "The American Dream is not a sprint or even a marathon, but a relay. It passes down from generation to generation." This is equally true of our individual stories. By depriving your audience of your story, you are also denying them the opportunity to grow from it. That is a missed opportunity for everyone.

## GREAT STORIES DO NOT REQUIRE GREAT STARTS

For the past few years, my company Key Ideas has worked with a nonprofit called Chrysalis Ministries, which has served more than 40,000 formerly incarcerated individuals. Their mission is to equip and empower these individuals—and their families—to overcome the consequences of incarceration. I met José in the Summer of 2019.[7] José was an athlete in high school and was always on the honor roll. After an ankle injury left him sidelined, he began to get bullied by a local gang. Rather than continue the abuse, José decided to join the gang for his own protection. Eventually, he was using and selling drugs for the gang. Between the ages of eighteen and twenty-four, José spent five years in jail for burglary and drug-related charges. As a teenager, José found himself in prison with grown men and again needed protection, so he soon became affiliated with the Texas Syndicate. The Texas Syndicate was started in the 1970s at Folsom Prison in California as protection from gangs like the Aryan Brotherhood and the Mexican Mafia. Los Zetas's drug cartel has been known to hire gangs like Texas Syndicate to carry out contract killings. This is not the kind of company you keep if you are trying to turn your life around.

After José was released, he began to carry a gun with him at all times because of the enemies he had made in prison. Before long, José was arrested for armed robbery and was facing thirty years in prison. "I started to realize that my way was not working," José shared in an interview with me. "While sitting in county jail facing those thirty years, I turned to the one thing I never had a lot of faith in, and that was God." José attended a prayer group for six months,

---

7   To watch the video we produced on José, you can visit https://vimeo.com/333630281.

praying not only for himself but also to ease the pain he had created for his family.

When I interviewed José's mom, she described, with tears rolling down her face, what it was like for her. "For me, it was like being in prison too. Me in prison outside, and him in. Just imagining what I never knew and what I will never know about what he really went through in there. Having to visit him, at first I was angry, then hurt, but at the same time full of love." When it was time for José to go to court, he was offered twelve years instead of thirty.

"The day that I signed for those twelve years, I felt like I signed a contract with God as well," José said. José was released from prison in January 2012. He now works for Texas Criminal Justice Coalition as a youth justice policy analyst in Austin, Texas. He had never stepped foot in the Texas State Capitol, but now he is a registered lobbyist. José regularly testifies to senators and House representatives advocating for incarcerated youth. Instead of running from his mistakes, he uses every opportunity he gets to share his story. Who better to advocate for criminal justice reform than someone who spent the better part of his youth behind bars? José has turned a painful past into a future full of purpose. He recently celebrated fifteen years of sobriety.

José's example shows that meaningful stories don't always come from the most comfortable places.

The most effective storytellers use the credibility they earned in the course of their lives to help them connect to their audience. When you can talk honestly and from the heart about your own experiences, and more importantly, when your audience can *see* that struggle reflected in your vulnerability and openness, your storytelling will become the most powerful tool at your disposal. Remember, " There is glory in your story."

## THE HARD STORY

We don't control all parts of our story, but we can control what we do with those parts. I have interviewed over 1,000 people in my career—people who have been homeless, addicted to heroin, and who have been abused in the worst ways. I once interviewed Michael Morton, who was falsely imprisoned for twenty-five years for killing his wife, only to be later exonerated by DNA evidence. My work has taken me as far as Liberia, Africa where I have had conversations with survivors of a two-decade-long civil war that left over 200,000 people dead. I have spoken with a mother in Chisinau, Moldova whose daughter had been sold into sex slavery. All these people share something very special. They have a story. A hard story. They are all choosing to take their worst experiences and use them for something good. To quote ten-year-old Rowan Windham, "If you're helping one person, then you're helping the world, and that is big!"

I had a chance to meet Rowan's mom last year. Rowan's

freckled face and fire-red hair could have easily been the image of any vintage Kellogg's cereal box. When he was eight years old, he learned that about one in four people in his hometown suffered from food insecurity. The summer months were the hardest for children living in poverty because they would no longer be provided the daily meals they got at school. Rowan decided to lead a food drive.

Rowan was extra special because he was spending time in the hospital for an incurable bone marrow disease called Shwachman-Diamond syndrome. Instead of gifts, he asked people to bring boxes of cereal. Much to the staff's surprise, Rowan ended up with 1,400 boxes of cereal that had to be carried out of his room on a dolly. Incredibly, Rowan's condition prevented him from ever trying cereal, since he was fed through a tube and IV for most of his life. Rowan used his story to advocate for kids who were facing huge challenges, even though those challenges were very different from his own.

Rowan was in need of a bone marrow transplant as a last-resort option, and he put out an all-call to people to join the marrow donation registry. People were so inspired by Rowan that thousands of people joined the registry. Sadly, Rowan never found his match, and in December of 2016, at the age of ten, Rowan passed. His mom continues to share her hard story to advocate for funding for medical research. In June of 2017, Methodist Hospital in San Antonio—where

Rowan spent much of his life—started the Rowan Windham Memorial Cereal Drive in partnership with the San Antonio Food Bank. That first year they raised enough cereal for 100,000 servings. In 2018, they made it to 120,000.

Rowan's mother's story resonated with me for so many reasons. It's a perfect example of someone sharing what is, undoubtedly, one of the most difficult human experiences in service of something bigger than herself. She allowed herself to be completely raw because helping others is what Rowan would have wanted. I've interviewed many people who have lost children, and for families going through such searing loss, it seems to be a source of comfort to know that the life of their departed loved one can, in a way, live through helping others.

Most of us have hard stories to share. I am originally from Sacramento, California. My parents divorced when I was five, so my sister and I bounced between the model home they had bought together and my Pop's bachelor pad. After several years of renting, my dad bought a house near Sacramento State University, where he was a professor.

My sister and I were the second set of kids from his second marriage. I have an older half-brother and two older half-sisters that I did not grow up near. My dad had all three of my half-siblings before he was twenty-five. He was forty when he had me. He was more established in his career, and I feel like we must have gotten the better dad version of him.

My dad was pretty big on taking us outside. One of my favorite memories of growing up was walking to the green belt near our house and exploring the winding dirt trails that led to the American River. Our ritual was to look for the best walking stick and collect an assortment of the fire-colored leaves that fell from a canopy of scarlet oak trees. We would walk to the river, though the neighborhood and the park were nearby.

I remember returning from one of our walks, and as my dad was taking off his tennis shoe, I noticed a circular scar near his ankle.

"How did you get that scar?" I asked.

"I got it when I was young," he said. "I went outside to play, and I had a rock stuck in my shoe."

"Oh, okay. Why didn't you just take it out?" I asked.

"I don't know. I guess I was just stubborn," he added.

That's my dad. I didn't think much about that story when I was little, but as I got older, I began to see it as a cautionary tale. We all tend to hang on to the things that hurt us a little longer than we should.

Holding onto something until it scars us is a dangerous

thing. We all have experiences in life that rock us to our foundation. We could choose to let those stories develop scar tissue in the dark. Or we can let them loose so they can light our path.

I would never encourage anyone to share a painful story before they are ready. What and when we share our story is a personal decision and should never be forced upon anyone who is not ready. The one thing I do know through my own experience, though, is that something divine happens when we share a hard story. Something beyond therapeutic. Perhaps a piece of ourselves that we get back, even in the midst of prodigious loss.

The Bible verse, John 10:10 says, "The thief comes only to steal and kill and destroy; I have come that they may have life and have it to the full." I believe that there is a God who wants us to live our best life. And when we share a hard story, not only are we living our best life, but we have an opportunity to help others live theirs.

Sketch Note Summary—Chapter 1

# Seek First to Understand

Diego Bernal was sworn into the Texas House of Representative District 123 on March 3, 2015. A proud product of San Antonio's Westside, Bernal understood better than most what an education could do for a child's upward mobility. He was born to a former farm worker and an educator. He and his sister were raised by his mom who believed in the power of a great education. The promise of a better life realized through education was a message that would stay with Bernal. He graduated from high school among the top of his class. He attended Michigan State, where he obtained a bachelor's degree, a master's in social work, and eventually a law degree. Bernal's life experience mixed with his education had prepared him well for his journey into public service.

His commitment to public education was anchored in two core beliefs. The first was that societal challenges like hunger, poverty, inadequate healthcare, affordable housing, criminal justice reform, unemployment, and crime can all be solved through education. The second was that, in order to realize education's fullest potential, it must be offered to every student fairly and equitably. A politician running on an education platform is about as novel as Mariah Carey popping up on a Christmas playlist or, say, a disappointed Dallas Cowboys' fan. What was uncommon is the approach that Representative Bernal took to understand the challenges children in his district faced.

Rather than leaning on his own understanding or relying on a consultant, he devised a plan to visit every single public school in his district and listen to the stories of the educators doing the work. This method would make any Dr. Stephen Covey disciple smile, as it embodies Habit #5 from the best-selling book, The 7 Habits of Highly Effective People: seek first to understand, then to be understood. Habit #5 is a must for every great storyteller who hopes to move people toward a desired outcome. Many of us stop short at trying to approach storytelling from a point of introspection. Your experiences alone shape your beliefs. The problem with that is not everyone has your experience. When we seek first to understand as storytellers, we make room for a more balanced perspective and a broader understanding of how to solve problems.

## A HISTORY OF SEGREGATION

Before discussing what Bernal learned, it is important to fully understand the district that he represents. Texas House District 123 includes fifty-five schools and three school districts, and it is one of the most economically diverse in the state. The concept of a diverse district is wonderful if it means that diversity exists within neighborhoods, but Bernal's district is the perfect example of a history of racism, which earned San Antonio the title of the most economically segregated city in the entire nation.

In 1936, maps created by Home Owners Loan Corporations (HOLC) reveal racially segregated neighborhoods in San Antonio. Those maps highlighted in red identified neighborhoods with high populations of African American and Latino residents as "definitely declining" or "hazardous." Anyone living in those neighborhoods were denied home loan mortgages, which also denied them the opportunity to build wealth through home ownership and revitalize declining infrastructure in their communities. Aside from not allowing people of color to invest in the revitalization of their neighborhoods, they were also unable to secure home ownership in more affluent areas. As San Antonio grew in the early decades of the twentieth century, Anglo families started to move outside the city center, creating suburbs. Many of these houses were deed restricted, meaning that no person of color could purchase land in this neighborhood. This policy of internal racial segregation happened for generations. In fact, it did not become illegal until the 1960s. This dark past has created residual challenges for the nation's seventh largest and third fastest growing city.

In the predominantly Hispanic neighborhoods west of downtown and the prominently African American neighborhoods to the east, there were smaller lots and more lots per block, which left little room for proper infrastructure. Sidewalks, drainage, lighting, and poor streets have made for substandard living conditions, and these neighborhoods have been redlined, or denied crucial services (either directly, or through exorbitant pricing).

A community health report released in 2016 by the Bexar County Health Collaborative revealed that citizens of San Antonio have a twenty-year life expectancy gap between the most impoverished zip codes and the most affluent ones. This shocking gap is only five years less than the life expectancy gap between Algeria, the African country with the highest life expectancy (seventy-five years) and Sierra Leone, which has the lowest life expectancy in the world (fifty years). The distance between Algeria and Sierra Leone is 1,600 miles, but the distance between San Antonio's poorest zip code, 78207, and wealthiest, 78257, is about twenty-two miles—a twenty-nine-minute Uber ride.

The inequities that exist in these neighborhoods naturally happen at a detriment to the public school system. Public schools in Texas are financed by a percentage of property tax dollars from the homes in the area that the school serves. Low property values, combined with a high percentage of government housing and an even higher percentage of renters, mean that the school districts serving historically impoverished neighborhoods of color have far less funding. Adding to the problem, San Antonio is deeply fragmented, with nineteen area independent school districts. The school districts that serve formerly redlined neighborhoods provide more social services and three daily free or reduced meals to 98 percent of the school population. Simply put, it costs more to educate students living in extreme poverty.

A pragmatic person might think school finance reform would be the first place to start. Bernal is a pragmatist, but he is equal parts realist. The Texas Supreme Court ruled that the public school finance system had met minimal constitutional requirements. Bernal still felt it was his moral obligation to find a way to improve public education. The only question is where do you start?

## GAINING UNDERSTANDING

Now that you have a basic understanding of what was happening in San Antonio, you might attempt to appreciate the herculean challenge facing Representative Bernal. Bernal, who had come from 78207 himself, saw it more as an opportunity. He believed that if he could find common challenges in different schools, different districts, in diverse neighborhoods; than there might be an opportunity to present solutions that would have sustaining impact across the state.

Bernal had a lot of insight on the situation, but the most transformational conclusion he came to was that he didn't know what he didn't know. I will say it again. He knew that he did not know what he did not know.

It would have been easy for Bernal to work on policy based on his experiences alone. Many of the schools Bernal visited were in or near the same neighborhoods he grew up in. He understood poverty. As a civil rights attorney he advocated and litigated on behalf of the working class, children, and immigrant communities. He was also a fighter. As a San Antonio city council member, he took on payday lenders by passing the strictest regulation in the state of Texas. There were many things he knew about the challenges facing the communities he represented. But he sought first to understand by hearing the stories of the educators who did the work every day. By doing so, he gained an insight that mixed with his own conviction, and it made for a mighty story-telling foundation.

He embarked on a learning tour without fanfare. No cameras, no media, no entourage beyond a few staffers. He also wanted to make sure that he created an environment where stories could be freely shared. No response would point back to any one educator or school, and his report would only include the ideas that came up consistently across every campus. This is what great storytellers do. They take the time to listen, reflect, and consider. Understanding challenges are easier when rooted in a personal experience, but you can't paint a complete picture if you never look beyond your own canvas. Going to the educators directly to ask questions took almost a year. But the understanding he gathered from the stories proved to be the best investment of time he could have made.

The educators shared the need for time for more quality instruction, more support staff, and a staffing plan that put the most experienced teachers in the schools with the most need. The most surprising obstacle came from one of his very first school visits. The principal had prepared a whiteboard with two columns. The first contained opportunities for growth, while the second included challenges. The first challenge on the list was food insecurity.

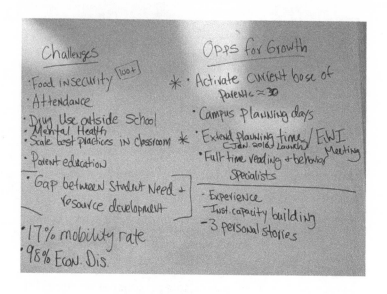

Challenges

- Food insecurity [100+]
- Attendance
- Drug Use outside School
- Mental Health
- Scale best practices in classroom ✱
- Parent education
- Gap between Student Need + resource development
- 17% mobility rate
- 98% Econ. Dis.

Opps for Growth

✱ · Activate current base of parents ≈ 30
- Campus Planning days
✱ · Extend planning time / EWI (Jan. 2016 launch) Meeting
- Full-time reading + behavior Specialists

- Experience
- Inst. capacity building
- 3 personal stories

Chronic hunger was a challenge echoed by every elementary and middle school that Bernal visited. Imagine being an educator trying to get a child to focus when she is hungry. That lack of focus can also lead to behavioral issues. According to Bernal, one leader said, "I didn't always know what to do with the hungry students who came to see me later in the day because we're not allowed to give them cafeteria food after the lunch period. There was one young man who came to see me more than a few times a week, so with him, I started walking back and forth between the main campus and one of the portables in the back. There was a pecan tree there, so we'd walk back and forth and stop so he could pick and eat a few until he felt better."

Another educator said, "There's a little girl, about seven, who walks herself four blocks to school every Monday. She comes early and waits right outside the door, waiting for it to open so she can run to the cafeteria and get breakfast. We know she doesn't get much food, or good food, on the weekends. We can tell."

As if it wasn't enough to work with kids not getting enough to eat, teachers pointed out that everything not consumed at lunchtime had to be thrown away. Imagine the frustration. You have hungry kids and an abundance of food in the same building, but overlapping district, state, and federal policies prohibit you from doing anything about it. According to Bernal, almost every campus throws away untouched, unopened, ripe, perfectly edible food every day.

Had Bernal not taken time to look for challenges beyond his own understanding, he would have surely missed an opportunity to address a problem that he did not even know existed.

The result was the Student Fairness in Feeding Act. House Bill 367 allowed schools to set up food pantries. This allowed schools to accept and store donated food and surplus food from the cafeteria. Students can either eat their food or put their uneaten food on the share table. The kids who need it most can take food home with them to be eaten at a later time. No questions asked.

This is the kind of common sense policy that would never

have been developed if a person in a position of influence did not make the time to listen before being heard. It also would not have been possible if the professionals who understood the challenges better than anyone else would not have been prepared to share their story. The outcome was not just impactful for the kids in their schools, their district, or even their city. The educators who shared their stories inspired a law that is, to this day, helping hungry students in the second-most food insecure state in the country.

Great storytellers seek first to understand. It is what Mr. Rogers did. When Mr. Rogers would invite a guest on his show, he would let the guest educate his audience. The same way he let Jeffery Erlanger educate the world on the rare condition that left him in a wheelchair. Like Rogers, Bernal asked thoughtful questions, put his subject in the position of influence, and through the process, educated and inspired. The result was a bipartisan effort to feed hungry kids all over the second largest state in the country. This is how movements are started.

## STORYTELLING CREATES MOVEMENT

Understanding is the first step to developing a meaningful story, but the work doesn't stop there. Bernal gathered data, listened to others' experiences, and came up with an action plan, but he still had to convince his fellow representatives. Data might be convincing, but it's rarely moving. Knowledge and facts only get you so far. People are more likely to take action when they feel something powerful, and that's where stories come in. Bernal's visits gave him a great deal of understanding, which he then transformed into stories— stories that moved his fellow representatives, regardless of their political affiliations.

As a Democrat in a predominantly red state, Bernal easily could have had his ideas dismissed if they were based in his own experience, or even in data, which can often be reinterpreted. That's why deciding to talk to educators directly was a stroke of genius. No matter what political party you subscribe to, you are going to have a much harder time ignoring the stories of more than fifty-five educators who have dedicated their entire career to serving students. Especially when they are saying the same thing across a very economically diverse district. When Bernal's bill was brought before the Texas Legislature, it could have met any number of obstacles, but because it was steeped in understanding, it was harder to dismiss.

In a blog post about the bill called "What They Said," Bernal wrote, "I view this document as a blueprint for nonpartisan, common sense education policy in Texas, both in terms of practical action items and school finance priorities. During my visits I didn't find Democrats or Republicans, conservatives or liberals; I found only people who wanted the best for our students." Bernal patiently gathered understanding, and then he told stories that spoke to people's hearts. He painted a compelling—and honest—picture of educators struggling daily with hungry children. These stories had a powerful emotional effect, and a movement was born.

This meaningful win during Bernal's first term built the momentum necessary for an even bigger breakthrough during his second term. As Vice Chair of the House Committee on Public Education, Bernal played a major role in introducing an $11.6 billion School Finance Reform Bill. House Bill 3 injected $6.5 billion into Texas schools, elevating funding per student by 20 percent, delivering pay raises to teachers statewide, and funding full-day Pre-K education. By seeking first to understand, Bernal gained the credibility that put him in a unique position to make an even greater impact.

In Bernal's case, the most impactful moment came when he learned that teachers' challenges weren't limited to money, training, or classroom resources. They had to do with the very real, immediate effects of food insecurity. If Bernal and those educators hadn't taken the time to create an inventory of challenges and opportunities, innumerable students might still be going through their days with empty stomachs.

Although Bernal was the one in a position of power, the educators he spoke with played a vital role. Had they not been prepared to share their stories, an opportunity to change a huge bureaucratic system would have been lost.

A well-prepared story, deployed at the right time, just might lend perspective to a person who can change everything.

Sketch Note Summary—Chapter 2

CHAPTER THREE

# Miguel's Gift

I met Miguel in high school. It was an awkward beginning. He was dating my sister. One day I came home from work, and there he was, this geeky guy with *Can't Buy Me Love* hair,[8] sitting next to her on our couch. She told me his pickup line had been, "I wonder what it would be like to kiss you?"

Some pickup line. I never asked if it worked. Some things are best left unknown.

As the years went on and his relationship with my sister took the inevitable course most teenage crushes take, I never thought I would see him again. Little did I know that Miguel

---

8   For those of you who aren't old like me, *Can't Buy Me Love* is an 80s movie starring a young Patrick Dempsey. You might know him as "McDreamy."

would not only become a friend but would give me a piece of advice that would completely change my life.

The next time I saw Miguel he had gotten a job as a cook in a comedy club. It was part of his dream to become a standup comedian. Fearful of the stage at first, he dipped a toe into the waters of the comedy pool with that kitchen job, happy simply to be in the atmosphere of the club. He had worked as a cook in the army, so this was a comfortable first step where he could study, build relationships with seasoned acts, and contribute to America's obesity problem.

Little by little, he eased his way onto the stage. At first, he performed in matinees where green comedians could get some reps and experienced comics could try out new material. These shows were tough. It is hard to make people laugh in the middle of the day. Many people were there just to escape the South Texas heat on their way to or from the historic Alamo across the street. The locals would come to the matinee to kill time before their movie started across the hall. Miguel was finding his way as a standup comedian, and the first time I saw him it was rough. It was bad. Bad Miguel, bad crowd, bad nachos, just bad.

It didn't take Miguel long to improve, and the next time I saw him perform, he killed it. His signature joke featured Arnold Schwarzenegger trapped inside a jack-in-the-box... He would slowly mimic the sound of the jack-in-the box handle turning, and just when it was getting uncomfortable, he would deliver, in a spot-on Terminator voice, "I could not *breathe* in there!"

Every time I'd see him, it stirred in me the desire to try it myself. "Man, I really want to do this," I'd say, and he'd encourage me to go for it. I worked up the courage once and told a few jokes during a freshman orientation to about 200 people. I am sure it was awful, but I managed not to make a complete fool out of myself. I scratched an itch, but it would be years before I ever hit the stage again.

## I GET A ROOMIE

One night at a bar, where we were hanging out before a midnight show at the comedy club, our mutual friend, James, told me that Miguel was going to ask to rent one of the rooms in my house. I had separated from my wife, and James had already started to stay in a room in the back of my house.

When he got around to asking, Miguel, as usual, made a lame pitch.

"Hey man, I heard you're getting divorced. Want a roommate?"

That's Miguel's personality. Straight and to the point. No bedside manner whatsoever.

Miguel moved in, and I suddenly had two roommates during the most difficult transition of my life. Overnight, the house where I started my family was converted into a halfway house for struggling comedians and broken dreams. Sounds like an Adele song, I know.

Elijah's mom and I shared custody of him. Luckily, he was too young to be traumatized by the smell of three bachelors and a steady diet of Kielbasa sausage and Ramen noodles. At least, I hope.

Having Miguel and James in the house really helped me pass the time without my son. I would go see them perform, and my desire to get on stage would only grow. I would watch them from the back of the stage, and I wanted to make people laugh like they did. I was jealous. I was like the unattractive Hemsworth brother. If that is a thing…You get the idea…

Comedy was something I had a burning desire to try ever since I watched the first "Comic Relief" special hosted by Robin Williams, Whoopie Goldberg, and Billy Crystal. I filled my free time going to Miguel and James's shows. The urge to try my hand at performing grew and grew. In a fit of inspiration, I stayed up all night and wrote a bunch of material. Great stuff, I knew. Killer stuff. I'd skip those awkward first steps and go straight to assured pro.

## A LESSON IN STORYTELLING

After I put together a good amount of material, I gave it to Miguel, confident that the next thing I would hear would be howls of laughter. I was so confident in the material, I went back to my room and waited to be knighted with a microphone or some other symbol of comedic brethren.

I waited...and waited...

And waited some more.

Finally, when minutes had extended into hours and I couldn't take it anymore, I knocked on his door.

"Hey! Did you read what I wrote?" I asked.

"Yeah."

"And?" I wanted to know.

"That was terrible."

I wondered if I'd heard him wrong, but he said it again, "That was awful."

Comedians are great at making you laugh, but they also have a knack for tossing little spears of truth. It *was* bad. That day I got my first lesson in stand-up comedy writing.

Stunned as I was by his seemingly callous assessment of my hard work, he offered me some priceless advice.

"If you're really serious about this," he began, "what you need to do while you're writing is to be honest. Write about yourself. That way, it'll always be original. Nobody has your exact story. If you write about your own experiences, real, authentic stuff that's happened to you, it won't sound like what every other comedian's talking about."

## KEY IDEA: BE AUTHENTIC

Original storytelling begins with just telling it like it is.

I took this to heart because comedians are among the best storytellers that exist. They have a gift for simplifying complex issues and eliciting an emotional response in a finite amount of time.

The more I thought about Miguel's advice, one thing became clear to me: when you perform your material, if it comes from an authentic place inside you, you'll deliver it with confidence and passion. Miguel's message was simple. I needed to build my material on a framework of authenticity, which meant mining the current state of my life for comedy.

This was hard.

I was going through a divorce. It was a painful experience. I wracked my brain over and over, looking for a way to make people laugh about something so personally painful. I was broken actually. I really wanted my marriage to work. My parents were divorced, and it killed me that that would be Elijah's story too. In hindsight, I probably should have been in therapy, but comedy was much cheaper.

Humorist David Sedaris says at the end of his Master Class, "I divide the world into two groups of people. There are those who pay someone to listen to their problems. And there are those who get paid to tell about their problems. I am very fortunate to be in group number two."

Once I committed to Miguel's advice, the material just flew out of me.

"So, I'm going through a divorce. I wanted to work things out, but her boyfriend wasn't willing to compromise. 'Come on, let me see her Wednesdays and every other weekend. Maybe a month during the summer.'"

It actually felt good. After that it was hard to contain myself. The jokes after that came streaming faster than season three of *Stranger Things*. Nobody in my family was safe.

"Everybody tries to give you advice when you are going through a divorce. Especially my dad. He said, 'Son I want to talk to you about your marriage.' I said, 'No offense dad, but you have been divorced twice. I am not listening to you.' My dad actually had some good advice, though. He said, 'Son, what you need in a good marriage is honesty... The truth will set you free.' That actually made a lot of sense to me...So the next time my wife came into the room and asked if the dress she was wearing made her look fat, I remembered what my dad said. I told her, 'No, that dress doesn't make you look fat...It's the way that you eat that makes you look fat. Also, the lack of exercise.' My dad said the truth would set me free, and he was right. She left.

My signature bit arose after I finally and truly tapped into the most authentic (and painful) part of my life as it was at that time.

"I'm a single dad, and any single dad will tell you that if your kid doesn't get what they want, they automatically start crying for their mom. I was like, 'OK, I'm not going to get mad at him. I'm just going to talk to him.'"

"I said, 'Son, I know you miss your mommy. But Mommy doesn't live here anymore.'"

"He's like, 'Why daddy?'"

"I said, 'Well, mommy and daddy stood in front of a room full of all our friends and family, and Mommy vowed before

God to be with Daddy 'til death do us part. But see, Daddy's still alive, honey. And that's right. Mommy lied to God..."'

This joke is what differentiated me, but it also connected me with every person in the audience that had a similar experience. It was thoroughly and completely my own story, which no one else was telling or could have told. Sharing my authentic story, even in a humorous context, connected me to a large audience immediately. Because what makes us unique also connects us.

My story especially connected me to men and women who had themselves experienced divorce or grew up with divorced parents. These folks were the ones laughing the hardest. It was relatable. Talking about your own story and being original can be the one thing that differentiates you from anyone else, while simultaneously connecting you with an audience.

It is one of the most powerful truths in life I've ever learned.

### CREATIVITY ROOTED IN AUTHENTICITY

Authentic storytelling comes from a place of truth, if not an objective, absolute version of it. There are aspects of "Mommy lied to God" that just didn't happen. I never actually told my son that Mommy lied to God. Elijah is almost seventeen now, and he has never seen me perform. In fact,

I just told him the joke for the first time a few months ago, only because this book was coming out.

Even though I didn't actually tell Elijah his mommy lied to God, the concept for the joke was rooted in truth. I really was going through a divorce. It wasn't something I just made up to connect to an audience or further my career.

There's the old saying that "Comedy equals tragedy plus time." In my work helping people craft and tell their authentic stories, I always say we are guided by the rule of "creativity balanced with authenticity."

You can be as creative as you want. You can approach your story in as many different ways as you want, as long as the story you tell is weighted and rooted in authenticity and truth.

For individuals, this idea manifests in different ways. In business, we ask our clients, "What do you want to be famous for? What sort of stake do you have in the ground? What flag are you going to plant and say, 'This is who I am?'" Those are the questions to answer that will point to what is authentic in your corporate tale.

The first pitfall is trying to tell the story you think your audience wants to hear, instead of the one you authentically have to tell. For example, a lot of the work we do at Key Ideas is with mission-driven nonprofits. These are wonderful organizations doing important work. But when I ask them what they're about, often we hear the same thing.

"We're providing hope."

This is a noble and worthy aspiration, but it's hardly a unique starting point for anyone to tell their story. There are as many people in San Antonio looking to provide hope as there are restaurants selling breakfast tacos.

These folks are telling the truth, but they're telling it in a very unoriginal way. There are many organizations selling hope for a lot longer than you, for one thing. Inevitably, unoriginality reveals its presence through buzzwords and clichés that drain any story of real meaning. These are the people who, when they *do* relate their story, something doesn't feel real.

This is a real challenge in any industry, but it's especially difficult for nonprofits. The nonprofit sector is addressing some of the biggest societal challenges that exist, but they can be terrible at sharing their own story. At least, not in a way that sets them apart.

If you don't believe me, I would like to present Exhibit A.

# EXHIBIT A:

Nonprofit Logos Brought to You by Samesies

This is a collection of nonprofit logos I collected over time. When I met leaders from these organizations, I took their business cards. I started to create a stack on my desk, and every time I met someone with a similar logo, I added it to the pile.

These logos all look like the crosswalk guy is doing yoga. Did all of these organizations get a Groupon to get a logo designed by some disgruntled Vistaprint graphic designer?

Do you see the problem with the lack of authenticity? All of these organizations are competing for the same limited resources in the same market. Their development directors are attempting to build relationships with the same donors, some of whom may not be familiar with their work. These nonprofits have boards that task their leadership with raising millions of dollars a year, just to be sustainable, but they won't let them spend thousands to develop a brand that clearly differentiates them.

There is glory in these organizations' stories, and they need to be shared in an authentic way. This extends to their logos, websites, videos, PowerPoints, and every other platform they leverage to deliver their message.

If you feel like you're having trouble figuring out what your original idea is, then it can help to get a fresh perspective. It can be extremely helpful to talk to the people you serve. They can often tell your story better than you can. People who have benefitted from your organization will often have a different way of talking about you than the people who perform that work every day.

Whatever your approach, as a storyteller you should strive to find what is unique about you and your organization—as long as it is honest and true. In storytelling, there is always a little bit of creative license. However, my company, Key Ideas, would never develop a concept that says something about a client that isn't authentically true. We believe in this so much that "creativity rooted in authenticity" is one of our core values. I suggest that you make it a core value too.

People have a knack for sniffing out a phony. When I was a youth pastor, a friend once said, "Kids can tell if you are being authentic right away. They don't need you to be cool. They just need to know you care." When we are authentic in our storytelling, not only do we honor our own story, but we show our audience respect.

## MIGUEL'S GIFT

I'll end this chapter with the same guy who got it all started.

Miguel.

The night that Miguel asked if he could be my roommate was actually the night of my birthday. It was a Saturday night, and we had decided to go barhopping. My friends James and Miguel would usually perform at the free midnight madness show that would run from 12-2 a.m. at the River Center Comedy Club. Imagine a captive audience of the finest—and drunkest—crowd your city has to offer. That night I convinced James and Miguel to skip the show and hop to the next bar with me and some other friends.

Not even one beer into the next bar, Miguel noticed a man sitting with a small group of people. He nudged me.

"Hey man, that's Paul Rodriguez."

Rodriguez is an old-school comedian, and in his time, he was one of the most well-known Latino comics. He'd been in movies and had a huge following, which included Miguel, one of his most ardent fans.

"He's the reason I got into comedy," he said once I confirmed his suspicions that the man in the corner was, in fact, the famed comedian. He kept pacing back and forth. He was giddy. I was afraid he was going to go up to him with the same line he gave my sister, "I wonder what it would be like to kiss you."

I told him that he should go talk to him. In hindsight, what I was really saying to him was, "Tell him your story."

At that point, Miguel's star was on the rise. He'd appeared on television a couple of times and had toured around the US. He hadn't made it by any means (he was still staying in my extra bedroom, after all), but he was doing pretty well.

Miguel took my advice and approached Rodriguez. In their brief conversation, Miguel thanked Rodriguez and told him he was the inspiration for Miguel's career. Miguel was vulnerable in that moment. He could have kept his story to himself. He could have come up with something inauthentic and tried to wow Rodriguez. Instead, he told his authentic story without any thought beyond connecting with someone he greatly admired.

It would be a great story even if it just ended there, but it didn't. Rodriguez was moved by Miguel's authenticity and connected instantly to his story. I don't know if perhaps he saw something of himself in the younger comic standing before him or if he felt a connection to their shared heritage. Whatever it was, Miguel's story had consequences he never could have dreamed up.

The Majestic Theater is one of the most beautiful and historic theaters in San Antonio. It is a special place. It opened in 1929, and it's recognized as one of the most beautiful, atmospheric theatres in the entire country. Legendary comedians like George Burns, Bob Hope, and in recent years, Jerry Seinfeld have performed there.

"I have a show at the Majestic tomorrow night," he told Miguel. "How would you like to open for me?"

And just like that, up-and-coming comedian Miguel was opening for his hero in one of the most treasured rooms in the entire country. All because of a story. All because of his willingness to tell that story, even when he wasn't going for a payoff. Telling that story put Miguel on the path to play the 3,000-seat theater of his dreams.

I was in the audience that night, laughing along with the rest of the crowd. When I think of that night now, what I remember most is Miguel's excitement afterward. He'd had an amazing set, and he knew it. I'd never seen him so happy.

About six weeks after that amazing night at the Majestic, I got a call from James telling me Miguel had collapsed while running in his hometown about forty-five minutes away from San Antonio. He died. He was thirty-two years old and in good shape, but he still died of a heart attack. I took a little comfort in knowing I had a small role in him eventually getting to open up for his idol. The gift I would get in return I am still benefiting from today.

We had a benefit for Miguel and his family at the comedy club. All the friends he had made as a comic went up on stage and gave him a posthumous roast. I had an opportunity to tell a few stories about him. A few months later, a local booker came up and said, "I saw you at Miguel's benefit show. You were funny. I want to book you." That was my first show. That was when I first took the time to take Miguel's advice and write the material about my divorce. The lesson Miguel taught me about bringing power to your stories simply by being authentic is the greatest piece of wisdom about stories and storytelling I ever received, and I have based a life and career on it.

A few other things happened as a result of learning to share my story. We will get to those later.

Sketch Note Summary—Chapter 3

# CHAPTER FOUR

# Aim for the Heart

O ur stories have the power to change the world. Social media platforms have given every human with access to a smartphone a voice and the prospect of a global audience. Never in our history have we been more connected.

As the late, great theologian Stan Lee wrote, "With great power, there must also come great responsibility." (This quote from the first Spider-Man story has always stuck with me…Sorry for the pun. I can't always help it…) It would be amazing if everyone chose to use the power of connectivity for good. Unfortunately, online, many people choose to focus on what they are against instead of what they stand for. With a 24/7 news cycle and access to multiple platforms, it also means if we don't get our story right, we can become famous for all the wrong reasons.

## THE FAILED FRUITERÍA

There are pitfalls to being inauthentic that are far worse than simply not connecting with an audience. In the previous chapter, we discussed the importance of creativity balanced with authenticity. That balance can actually make the difference between having a business, organization, or dream that thrives and one that never gets off the ground.

Jennifer Niezgoda clearly had a heartfelt love for the fruitería, a staple of traditional Mexican culture. Niezgoda is a well-known travel Instagrammer and blogger who markets herself as the "Barefoot Bohemian." Her personal brand is about seeing the world, bringing her love of different cultures to life, and celebrating them—all worthy goals. In this way, Jennifer was authentic.

After returning from a trip to Mexico in 2017, though, she had a brainstorm: she was going to modernize the concept of the fruitería and drag a time-tested treasure of Mexican culture into the twenty-first century. She decided to open her own modern fruitería in San Diego's Barrio Logan, a traditionally ethnic neighborhood already struggling with homelessness and gentrification.

She called it "La Gracia."

She opened a Kickstarter campaign to raise money for the venture. In a cringeworthy video, the blonde-haired-blue-eyed social media influencer cavorted in stylish clothes through Barrio Logan, backed by a soundtrack of strumming Spanish guitars. She blithely included footage of herself in front of murals depicting Latino heroes, and she described Barrio Logan as "San Diego's most vibrant, up-and-coming neighborhood." People who donated, she added, would have the chance to bring "a healthy option to the Barrio," all of which suggested that she discovered a neighborhood without a rich and worthy history of its own.

In her enthusiasm, Niezgoda had not done the research that might have told her that her plan was not bound for success. Though not malicious, she was tone-deaf to the feelings of the residents who already lived there. She was overenthusiastic about her latest passion and didn't adequately consider the audience that would buy into it.

Her opening line was, "Above all places, Mexico stole my heart." Then her voice rises an octave, and she says, "And then I found it here! In San Diego!"[9]

As you might imagine, this did not go over well. Niezgoda faced a storm of criticism from neighborhood activists and residents. The Kickstarter video went viral for all the wrong

---

[9] As if one day she was following her friend to the new hot yoga place downtown, and that bitch left her at a yellow light...So she ended up taking a wrong turn, and all of a sudden...Holy shit! There is Mexico next to that Dollar Tree!

reasons. Soon after, the campaign was shuttered, and Niez-goda's idea died with it.

Bottom line, there was a total disconnect between the person who was the face of the Kickstarter campaign and the community it sought to serve. When you're crafting your story, there are moments where you need to ask yourself, *Is this really a great measure of who I am? What is my experience? What makes me uniquely qualified to tell this story?*

Most importantly, check your motivation. *Why do I want to tell this story?* In the case of La Gracia, Niezgoda likely didn't do any of these things.

The moral of the story isn't that a white woman can't go into a Latinx neighborhood and start a business that brings value to the neighborhood and serves the community. The biggest problem with Niezgoda's failed fruitería was that the brand and persona she brought to the enterprise did not feel authentic, and because of that, the community expunged her before she could even get the project underway. I don't think she understood that going on vacation in Mexico wasn't a sufficient basis for bringing a business back to a predomi-nantly Latinx neighborhood. She didn't do her research or understand her demographic.

## A BURRITO BOWL OF EMOTION

Let's contrast this with the startup story of Steve Ells, the founder and former CEO of Chipotle Mexican Grill. For the longest time, I avoided eating at a Chipotle restaurant. I had nothing against the chain, but it just seemed sacrilegious considering all of the incredible Tex-Mex restaurants in San Antonio. On my side of town, you can throw an avocado in any direction, and it will turn into guacamole before it hits the ground. That is how many Mexican restaurants I have in a two-mile radius. Chipotle was just not on my short list of places to visit.

That was before I learned their story.

One night, I was at home watching a Netflix series on the origins of high-profile businesses. One of the episodes focused on Chipotle, and even though I had never given Chipotle a second thought before, by the end of the episode, I was craving it. How had that happened?

They got me invested in their story.

The story behind the company had tugged at my emotions and connected me to the brand in a new, deeper way. When someone can successfully explain their "why," they have an opportunity to turn doubters into brand evangelists.

I had just finished producing a video for the Culinary Institute of America (CIA), one of the world's foremost cooking schools. There are three campuses across the country: New York, Napa Valley, and San Antonio. It is the Harvard of culinary schools, and many of its alumni have gone on to win James Beard Awards or work in Michelin Star-winning kitchens. Famous chefs, including Anthony Bourdain, Cat Cora, and Rocco DiSpirito, are all CIA Alumni. I was intimately familiar with the hard work and vision that came out of that place.

The show explained how Ells, a graduate of the New York campus of CIA, had dreams of starting his own high-end restaurant, but he lacked the kind of money it takes to open a place like that. In the documentary, he says, "The reason I opened Chipotle was to generate enough cash so I could afford to open a full-scale restaurant."

With a loan from his dad, Chipotle was born. Ells didn't have much money, so he used inexpensive materials to furnish the restaurant. Barn metal lined the restaurant. They used plywood for the chair backs, and pipes made up the table legs and stools. The environment Ells created was consistent with the food he served. He developed a menu around locally sourced foods.

Ells's backup plan was wildly successful from the start. Within one month, he was selling 1,000 burritos per day. His story resonated with people because it was rooted in his authentic experience. He had started this restaurant as a way to reach another, loftier goal: a fine dining restaurant. But he hadn't compromised his values, and he created a quality product that was a fresh, relatively inexpensive alternative to fast food.

He didn't make a promo video with Spanish guitars, where he salsa dances into frame and says, "You know what the barrio needs? Some healthy options! How about some farm-to-table barbacoa and tofu, bitches?" Unlike Niezgoda, Ells hadn't gone into a community with a rich past, only to impose his own vision. Chipotle wasn't trying to compete with the local mom-and-pop taqueria. The restaurant was filling another niche, and it was coming from a place of authenticity, not presumption. Ells had made his own category, and to a large degree, that's what made his restaurants a success.

When I finally learned about Ells's story, it connected with me. My work for the CIA made Ells relatable, and suddenly a restaurant that until then I had been chilly toward became one of my favorites. I liked the food, but I *loved* the story behind it even more.

## ELEPHANT AND RIDER

At the very least, storytelling has the power to convert apathy into appreciation. If you want more than appreciation though—if you're aiming for a movement—I suggest you aim for the heart.

## KEY IDEA: FIRST HEART, THEN HEAD

Author John Kotter wrote in his book, *A Sense of Urgency,* "Martin Luther King, Jr. did not reduce anger among blacks and contentment and anxiety among whites by announcing on the Washington Mall, 'I have a strategic plan.'"

Instead, he told a story that aimed straight for the heart. He told it so well that his message inspired a movement. Martin Luther King showed that the poor treatment of blacks was inconsistent with America's long-cherished values. He also appealed to Christians, arguing that harmful behavior to blacks undermined Christianity itself. Kotter explains, "Mindless emotion is not the point. Generally, the challenge is to fold a rational case directed toward the mind into an experience that is very much aimed at the heart."

Or, you could say that he was speaking to both the elephant and rider.

The scholars Chip and Dan Heath explain why aiming at the heart is so effective in their book, *Switch: How to Change Things When Change Is Hard.* The conventional wisdom in psychology is that the brain has two independent systems at work at all times. First, there is what we call the emotional side. That's the part of you that is instinctive, that feels pain and pleasure, and that watches *Grey's Anatomy* and *This Is Us*. The second is the rational side. It is the analytical part that likes to plan for the future and thinks that The Container Store holds the answer to all life's problems.

The authors refer to the work of the psychologist, Jonathan Haidt, who compares the emotional side to an elephant and the rational side to a rider. Perched atop the elephant, the rider holds the reins and seems to be the leader, but the rider's control is only so powerful compared to a six-ton emotional elephant.

Your rider says, "We need to get out of debt," but your elephant says, "but we work hard, and we deserve a new car." The rider says, "We should really get some rest," but the elephant says, "just one more episode of *Stranger Things...*"

This concept explains why change can be so hard. We always have internal conflict with ourselves. And when our rational side is up against our hefty emotional side, the rider does not stand a chance.

## KNOWING IS HALF THE BATTLE

It is no different for an audience. They need to be moved in a way that goes beyond reason and logic. Knowing is not enough. Or if it helps, maybe remember it as, knowing is only half the battle.

Do you remember the cartoon *G.I. Joe*? Not the Channing Tatum *G.I. Joe*. I'm talking about old-school *G.I. Joe*. After every episode there was a public service announcement. Something like, "If a creeper driving a minivan offers you candy, don't take the candy. Run...Remember, don't jump in the van, boys and girls!" Then, G.I. Joe would come out and say, "Now you know, and knowing is half the battle." But they would never tell you what the other half of the battle was! So frustrating!

Well, that is how your audience will feel if you don't create content that drives emotion. Either consciously or subconsciously, your audience will feel cheated. Don't leave your audience with only half the battle. Don't just give them all of the practical reasons they should choose you. It is just not enough to know what you should do. People need to feel something to experience a transformation or sustainable change. Remember, first heart, then head. Elephant, then rider.

Maya Angelou put it best: "I have learned that people will forget what you said, people will forget what you did, but they will never forget how you made them feel." People pay to be moved. We buy books, go to movies, and stream our favorite music because of how it makes us feel. The best storytellers understand how to make their audiences feel something, largely by connecting their own experiences to the storyteller's tale.

This perspective is not shaped only by abstract ideas; it's based on my own life. In the last chapter, I shared my personal journey, which significantly changed when I shared my authentic story on stage. That process of actively telling my story had a few major side effects...

At that time, I was a total mess. Writing about my divorce was like therapy because I could talk about my problems and make other people laugh. After only three months of doing stand-up, I remember doing a show in front of 2,000 people, and I did a great job, but I vividly remember crying the whole way home. I was still going through all the things that I was talking about on stage. I believed at that point that I would never love again. But even though it was difficult, I continued to share my story every chance I got.

I started attending a place called City Church, which was exactly what I needed. It felt like each sermon was directed at me and my situation. The pastors were funny, which I appreciated, and they never shied away from being transparent about their own struggles. I did not feel judged at City Church, and because it was a safe space, I felt like the conditions for recovery were possible. I truly believe that when we are at our worst, God will put people into our lives that can breathe new life into us. I also believe that this time was important for me to learn how to let go of my anger and guilt and to start fostering a greater relationship with God.

I volunteered to operate the cameras at the church, and after a couple of years, I invited the arts pastor to come see a local late-night talk show I was producing. It sounds glamorous, but it was basically the real-life version of Wayne's World from SNL (with even less of a budget). By this time, the show had improved, but we were still filming in a hole-in-the-wall Italian eatery, and on the occasions when our guests canceled, we would literally interview someone eating at the restaurant.

I guess the arts pastor was impressed enough, because soon afterwards, he asked if I would help produce one church service per month. The first one was on Valentine's Day, and it was titled "Break Up/Divorce." It may seem odd, but whimsical lovebirds forget that Valentine's Day can actually be really hard for people who aren't in a relationship. Yeah, we are the ones giving you crazy, ugly looks when the florist delivers you a dozen roses at work.

Although I had been very transparent about my divorce on stage, most of the people I volunteered with at the church had never heard it. I first shared my story during a planning meeting for the "Break Up/Divorce" service, and the committee actually agreed to let me go on stage and do stand-up.

(They wouldn't let me change the service title to "Mommy Lied to God," but you have to pick your battles.)

The week of the service, I was at a school assembly watching my son sing a song with his kindergarten class. My ex-wife turned to me and said, "I'm thinking about checking out your church. What are the service times?"

I had to be honest, so I said, "You are totally welcome to come to church, but there's a disclaimer. If you come this weekend, I will be on stage talking about you." I gave her more context, but I had absolutely no expectation, after that, that she would come. The only time she had ever seen my material, it was because I had accidentally left some notes in Elijah's diaper bag before my first show. She called me fuming.[10]

So, yeah. I thought it was pretty certain that she wouldn't be there. The 8:30 service rolled around, then 10:00, and I didn't see her there. No sign of her at the 11:30 service. Then, much to my surprise, she came into the 1:30 service, visibly nervous. I assured her it would be fine. After all, I wasn't going to point to her in the audience and ask her to stand up and wave.

I told the "Mommy lied to God" joke, but I also talked about

---

10  Years later, she admitted that she read the material out loud to her mom, and her mom totally laughed.

learning how to forgive. I ended my talk by saying that I would no longer focus on the love I felt that my ex-wife had taken away but on the love she had given that could never go away. As I walked offstage, a picture of me and my son appeared on the screen.

After the service, my ex came up to me in tears and gave me a big hug. It was some much-needed closure. Since then, my relationship with Elijah's mom has not been perfect, but we both vowed to never put Elijah in the middle of any of our disagreements. He is not our therapist, nor is he a tool to get back at one another when we don't see eye to eye.

I also had many other people who came up to thank me for sharing my story. Many of them said they needed to hear the message because they were in the middle of a divorce or were still recovering from one.

I think that the message resonated because of how we structured our presentation. My pastor could have given all the biblical reasons for forgiveness. He could have cited lots of scripture and referred to ancient stories. He could have chosen to talk about the psychology behind forgiveness or referenced mainstream academic research. He could have started with a few buzzworthy quotes, like this memorable gem from Anne Lamott: "Not forgiving is like drinking rat poison and then waiting for the rat to die."

Actually, I am certain that the pastor did most of these things during the course of the service. But before any of that, he let a broken man on the road to recovery tell a few jokes and share his story.

He knew that emotion would speak to people better than any data or rational explanation ever could. He knew that true connections speak to the heart before they ever go for the head.

## NEW BEGINNING

Sharing my story that day was a pivotal point in my life. After the service, many came up to thank me. Some shared that they were still struggling with their own divorce, and the message came at the perfect time. A year later, I met someone who said she had been sitting with her mom and four-year-old son during that service. She had turned to her mom and said, "Guys like that don't really exist. I have never met a guy with that perspective." She said the message came at a really important time in her life when she was also still struggling with the collateral damage of her own divorce.

We started dating in the spring of 2010, and this November, we will be celebrating our ninth year of marriage. On our wedding day, my then seven-year-old son Elijah was my best man, and Jonathan, who was five, walked his mom down the aisle. It was the perfect day. Five years ago, we added a little spitfire to the family. Her name is Elyse, and she is as beautiful as her mom.

I don't tell this story because I think everyone going through a divorce should take a crack at stand-up comedy. In fact, performing at a hole-in-the-wall bar in Laredo, Texas can be quite the opposite of uplifting. I'm sharing because this shows just why I believe so strongly in the power of story-telling. It has changed my life.

Time and time again, I have interviewed people who have endured the worst parts of human experience. What they all share is the fact that they are sitting in a chair, using those experiences to help other people. They are using their hearts before their heads, and they are making meaningful connections with other people. That is beautiful.

Now when I look back at that difficult time in my life, I know that there was a purpose in my pain. I know that there is power in my story, and it is what drives me to want to help others share theirs. It is why I agreed to write this book.

Sketch Note Summary—Chapter 4

# CHAPTER FIVE

# Consistency

In March 2004, Senator John Kerry of Massachusetts took to the podium at an appearance at West Virginia's Marshall University as part of his campaign for President. He was looking to deny President George W. Bush a second term in office.

He had reason to be optimistic. Nearly three years removed from the terrorist attacks on the World Trade Center and Pentagon, public sentiment toward the ensuing wars in Afghanistan and Iraq had cooled as casualties and costs mounted. It had been almost a year since the President's infamous "mission accomplished" speech aboard the U.S.S. Abraham Lincoln, and victory—whatever that might look like—did not seem closer.

Kerry, a decorated Vietnam War veteran who had first come

to prominence in the early 1970s as a result of his very public opposition to the war, locked his party's nomination for President earlier that month and held a five-point lead in the polls in early March—50 percent to Bush's 45 percent.

On March 16, Kerry inflicted upon himself the first of what would become a drumbeat of wounds, which marked the final months of the campaign. During a question-and-answer session, Kerry was asked about his support for a 2002 resolution to add $87 billion to the federal budget to pay for military operations in Afghanistan and Iraq.

The question was a delicate one for Kerry, who did not want to appear too soft on terrorism but who also needed to retain his credibility as a candidate disinclined to plunge the country into more needless warfare.

His response changed the course of the campaign and American political history.

"I actually did vote for the $87 billion," he equivocated, "before I voted against it."

This line was a disaster of epic proportions. Though there was a lot of context to be considered in his reply, the electorate (and politics in general) did not care for context. Kerry opened himself up for the label of "flip-flopper," and Karl Rove and the rest of Bush's strategy team ran spot after spot that branded Kerry as someone whose actions were inconsistent with his beliefs.

Consistency is a key factor for every storyteller. Ironically, it was Rove's consistent message attacking Kerry's lack of resolve that eventually did Kerry in. The damage was instantly apparent. By the end of the month, Bush led Kerry 49 percent to 46 percent, and Kerry never regained his momentum. Political operatives dredged up myths about his military service and offered them up to a public already conditioned to question the consistency of Kerry's story. Bush cruised easily to victory in November, after Kerry's campaign endured death by a thousand cuts.

Kerry and his campaign learned the hard way that when it comes to storytelling, consistency is king.

## KEY IDEA: CONSISTENCY IS KING

Most of us will never run for office or become a political strategist, but we all have people we hope to influence. We take part in micro-campaigns all the time. A consistent message shows our audience that we know who we are and how we can be of service to them.

Consistency also has the power to put our audience at ease. Remember the way Mr. Rogers opened and closed his shows? By changing from his suit jacket to a cardigan and lacing up his tennis shoes. Mr. Rogers was a master at getting his audience to feel comfortable, thanks to established routines and messaging. Clear and consistent messaging should always be your goal. It is especially vital when working in a saturated marketplace.

## PERSONAL INJURY

American law schools pump out graduates every year at a rate that far exceeds demand. This lack of ready legal employment leaves tens of thousands of lawyers, both by choice and by necessity, to fend for themselves after graduation. One of the most lucrative areas of law focuses on personal injury disputes.

We have all seen the commercials. It really does not matter where you live. A guy yells at the TV at the top of his lungs, while riding on top of an eighteen-wheeler and claiming to be the toughest attorney in town. At times you wonder if you are watching a real commercial or if the channel accidently changed to the World Wrestling Entertainment Hour. There is just no way these guys didn't dream of being Hulk Hogan growing up.

I watched a lot of Hulk Hogan and the Ultimate Warrior as a child, but as a storyteller, I was not super excited about creating a campaign for a client that looked and sounded like everyone else. So, when I had an opportunity to produce a campaign for Steve, a personal injury attorney, I was really happy to learn that he had no interest in taking the path of so many of his competitors.

In one of our initial meetings I asked why so many attorneys advertised that way. He said they are targeting blue collar people with little education. The higher a person's education and the more money they make, the more likely they are to already know an attorney, or at least to have a friend or family member that could refer them to one. The rest of the population gets the WWE.

I couldn't help but get a little pissed about the fleet of attorneys that, for years, have been insulting the intelligence of the communities they serve. I knew I could never be a part of that, but I still had the difficult task of trying to differentiate my client among the sea of attorneys yelling on TV.

Our first task was to understand what was authentic and honest about Steve. We needed to dig into what was different about his practice and then creatively use those differences to help him craft a unique story. We also needed to understand what was important to the clients he served.

At Key Ideas, we offer a storytelling workshop that is a micro version of the large principles we cover in this book. In order to figure out how to differentiate Steve's law firm, we suggested he start with the workshop. We asked for a diverse representation of his team, drawing from every level of expertise, including partners, paralegals, and receptionists. In this workshop, we discovered three unique things that set Steve apart from the eighteen-wheeler warriors he was competing with: trust, experience, and passion.

These were all characteristics authentic to Steve that we felt a person who had just been in an accident would value in an attorney. Drawing on these traits, here are the three scripts we came up with (minus the call-to-action information at the end). See if you can tell how they differ from the other commercials you might see on TV.

## GREAT LAW FIRM

A great law firm is so much more than one man. A great law firm has a team of compassionate professionals who know the law and know how to make it work for you. At XYZ Law Firm, we strive every day to be a great law firm by putting you first, listening, answering your questions, and using our experience to get you results. If you or a loved one have been injured in an accident, call XYZ Law Firm...

LOGO
*Trust, Compassion, Experience*

## SERVICE

At XYZ Law Firm, it's our goal to provide you a higher level of service. We listen to you, find you help in difficult situations, answer your questions along the way, and do not rest until we get you results. We truly hope you will never need an injury attorney, but if you do, we are here for you. If you or a loved one have been injured in an accident, call XYZ Law Firm...

LOGO

*Trust, Compassion, Experience*

## WHO DO YOU CALL?

How do you decide which attorney to call after an accident? You don't want some TV character yelling at you. Or some out-of-town attorney you will probably never meet. At XYZ Law Firm, we put you first. We listen to you, answer your questions, and don't rest until we get you results. After an accident...

You get the idea...

The last was my favorite because we knew that our client did not have the same budget as some of the other attorneys on TV, and we wanted people to remember Steve when the other attorneys ran their more aggressive ads.

The ads were very successful. After they appeared, market research ranked our client's spots as two to three times more effective than those of his competition. He also compared the ads to previous spots he had produced, and on a ranking scale from 1-10, the ads were scoring eights and nines, where, previously, the highest he had scored was a four. The ads were different, but they were also consistent. They all looked like they were part of the same family, and they reinforced values that were important to the client, aside from just money and strength.

## THE CLASH

Steve got drawn into the shiny new idea syndrome. That's when someone gets a new idea and completely changes their messaging to connect to the new idea, instead of continuing to establish a consistent, authentic brand message that is already working. He started asking us to produce spots that had no connection to the core message we had developed. Moreover, the three signature traits—trust, experience, and compassion—were not reinforced anywhere else in his marketing. They weren't on his website, billboards, or client brochures.

Eventually, after months of internal conversations with my team, I decided to return the balance of our retainer and discontinue our work together. This was actually a really hard decision. Key Ideas was still a small operation and at the time, and I am pretty sure that was the only monthly retainer we had. But I didn't believe in the work that we were doing anymore. Sure, we had not defaulted to WWE spots, but I knew that we were not building the kind of consistent messaging that would have a sustainable impact.

Maybe I thought we would be able to quickly convert another personal injury attorney to our storytelling methodology. We haven't. I am still proud of the spots we created with Steve, and I learned a lot in the process. As Storysmith in Chief, my failure was not working enough on my relationship with the client to effectively convince him that changing the message too frequently was a really bad idea. I didn't drive home just how important consistency really is.

Once you've established messaging that works, stick with it. Consistency is king. The best brands don't change their messages every year, because constantly changing your message can pull people away from your brand. If your message changes every time your marketing director does, then you're doing it wrong.

Plus, you should make sure that your story is communicated consistently on every platform. Steve's website told a different story from his television ads, which told a different story from his print ads. Your brand should be consistent, so that no matter where someone sees it, they will receive the same message. How often have you picked up a business card from someone and gone to their website, only to find that it looks like the two things were created in different decades? If your business card was created when Obama was president, but your website is Clinton-era, then it's time for an upgrade. Every touchpoint where your customers might interact with your company needs to align and remain consistent.

## BRANDS THAT DON'T CHANGE

Coca-Cola is one of the most iconic brands in American history, if not the world. One of the keys to its success, year after year, is undoubtedly the consistency of the brand's iconography throughout its whole lifespan. Consider this:

1886                          1890                          1905

1940                          1950                          1969

1985                          1987                          1993

2003                          2007

Coca-Cola Logos, 1886–2007

There are variations on the theme, but for more than a century, Coca-Cola's message has remained largely consistent. The brand has changed very little over the decades.

Beyond the font and visuals, the *tenor* of Coca-Cola's message has also never wavered. The ads are upbeat. They always extoll the virtues of harmony and peace. Even their recent campaign for flavored Diet Coke features characters bemusedly sidestepping the unmentioned health concerns surrounding their sugary sodas. The ads tell the audience that the drinks, "Just make me feel good. Life is short." They might as well say, "If you don't drink Coke, the terrorists win. Why do you hate polar bears…and the world?"

The message of harmony and goodwill that Coca-Cola works so hard to send out into the world transcends demographics. If you go to Walt Disney World's Epcot, there is even a Coca-Cola-themed store, complete with soda fountains that dispense the many flavors the company produces around the world. While the flavors differ depending on regional tastes, the messaging behind the Coca-Cola brand remains the same:

Harmony.

Peace.

Good humor.

It is a winning combination, and the company has been well served by sticking to it. Their ads have rotated throughout the years, but their message has not.

## OWN YOUR CATEGORY

When we do not clearly define who we are and who we are for, our audience will put us into their own category. The category I owned as a comic was the bitter divorced guy. Hopefully your category is more appealing.

You can see companies successfully owning their categories in every industry.

USAA, the San Antonio-based financial services company, was founded in 1925 by a small group of Army officers looking to insure themselves when existing insurers refused their business (deeming them to be high-risk customers). In the decades since, the company has clearly defined itself in terms of what it's for and why it exists. It's about insurance, banking, and investing, but at the end of the day, USAA exists to help servicemen and women. They own their category, and that is a result of the story only USAA can tell.

They have one of the best taglines I have ever heard: "We know what it means to serve." It speaks to their commitment to outstanding service and their unique understanding of the men and women who risk their life for our country. This strategy of owning their category has grown USAA's annual revenue to $159 billion, as of 2018.

## UNIQUE SELLING PROPOSITION

Companies that successfully own their category embody the principles that Rosser Reeves, one of the greats in the history of advertising, discussed in his seminal 1961 book *Reality of Advertising*.[11] Reeves argues that every advertising campaign should have three elements, exemplified in the idea of the Unique Selling Proposition:

1. A specific benefit to the consumer for buying a particular product or engaging a specific service.
2. Whatever benefit you offer, it must be one that the competition cannot. It has to be something that consumers can *only* derive from your product.
3. The proposition needs to be strong enough to move the masses to action, and it must be something they really want.

Reeves was a pioneer in advertising. For fans of *Mad Men*, he was one of the inspirations behind John Hamm's character, Don Draper. The idea of the Unique Selling Proposition (USP) is an important one because it aligns nicely with the idea that your story is the most important thing you own.

Find your USP if you don't already know what it is. Maybe

---

11  Rosser Reeves is the ex-Chairman of the Board of Ted Bates & Company. He developed the slogan for M&M's, "Melts in your mouth, not in your hand." He is one of the few people elected to the Advertising Hall of Fame.

you know what it is, but you are watering down your message by trying to be too many things to too many people.

Your story tells people, customers, or the HR person interviewing you for a job what specific benefits hiring you will bring.

Your story lets everyone know what it is that you can do that no one else can offer.

Your story, by connecting with your audience's emotions, can move people to action.

Putting your USP to use requires a consistent message, told frequently, across every platform where it finds a home.

## DON'T STOP CREATING

Organizations might spend tens of thousands of dollars creating content one year, and then they think they are good for the next five. Not only will that minimize your opportunity to attract new customers, it increases the likelihood that you will lose the ones you already have. You might think this is because you can't afford to create content every year when the truth is, you can't afford not to. Jia Wertz, a contributor to *Forbes-Woman* wrote recently, "It can cost five times more to attract a new customer than it does to retain an existing one." She also cites research conducted by Fredrick Reichheld of Bain

& Company, which shows that increasing customer retention by just 5 percent can increase profits by 25-95 percent.

Years ago, I was working with the executive director of a school foundation that funds, among many things, innovative school grants for teachers. The teachers and programs funded are very diverse, and we created a series of videos to highlight them. One video in particular highlighted a small grant for a strings program. Basically, an elementary school music teacher received enough money to buy his students some instruments. The teacher was enthusiastic, and the kids were cute. The grant had been funded by a small $10,000 donation from a foundation. After the video was complete, the executive director sent it to the foundation with a thank-you note. Within an hour, the donor emailed back and said, "This is wonderful. Let's talk about expanding this program district-wide." The $10,000 turned into $100,000, all from a carefully crafted story and a thank you.

Think of yourself as Netflix in a world of streaming storytellers. If you want people to continue to "subscribe" to your work, you have to continue to reach them. Sure, you will always have a percentage of people that come back for the classics, but you still need to come up with original content. That content should be new but consistent with your message and the category you own.[12]

---

12 It is not enough to invest in a marketing director to create content if they have no real budget to do it with.

## SIMPLICITY

Consistency is key, but it's not the only part of effectively telling your story. The most consistent story can still be too complex or convoluted, and no one is drawn in by a confusing or overly complicated story. In the next chapter we will examine simplifying your message, and we'll explore how an unfettered message offered in clear, simple terms is one of the most underappreciated aspects of storytelling.

Sketch Note Summary—Chapter 5

# CHAPTER SIX

---

# Simplify

P ride comes before the fall.

If I'd only remembered that before my talk to that group of eighth graders, things wouldn't have gone sideways for me.

It was supposed to be an easy appearance. I've spoken in front of groups, large and small, literally hundreds of times. So, when my friend asked me to address her daughter's middle school graduation class, I readily agreed.

After all, what could go wrong? Her school was looking for a speaker who could bring substance *and* brevity to their talk, and I'd been a youth pastor, performed at comedy clubs, churches, and universities. I would go in there, give 'em a little dose of the "C-los," and be on my way.

Adding to my confidence, I had just successfully completed a PechaKucha night, and I had compressed a thirty-minute talk down to seven tight minutes. This gave my friend the idea that I'd be a good keynote speaker while the eighth-grade graduating class gobbled up their spaghetti dinner.

For the uninitiated, the PechaKucha movement (which translates roughly as "chit chat") began in 2003 at an architectural firm in Tokyo. They had an experimental studio space and needed a plan to attract designers and other creatives. The main tenet of PechaKucha is to keep your presentations short and fast-paced, and people responded to the format eagerly. The movement exploded, and now PechaKucha Nights (known as PKNs) are now held around the world. These short-form, energetic presentations are short enough to allow multiple speakers at any given event. Topics vary widely, but speakers often include artists, writers, and academics—basically, anyone with something to say and the ability to say it quickly, with style.

I had a busy week, so I figured I would just give my PechaKucha talk. I made no attempt to alter my presentation—a major flaw, especially considering the age difference between my usual audience and this group of middle schoolers. My plan, if you can call it that, was to wing it: just go in there and give my usual talk with nothing tailored to the crowd.

Big mistake.

Have you ever spoken in front of a gaggle of eighth graders? Turns out, it's an intimidating bunch. They did not want to be there, and they didn't care one bit about who I was or what I was there to communicate to them.

Comedian John Mulaney has a bit where he says he can't stand thirteen-year-olds because their insults are really accurate. They have a way of finding the thing you are most sensitive about, and then they go straight for it. He's right.

Needless to say, I bombed.

After my "Mommy lied to God" joke didn't work, I quickly became a browner version of Chris Farley's character, the motivational speaker Matt Foley, who was always overcaffeinated and blurting nonsense about living in a van down by the river. My story about my divorce did not make any connection to these middle schoolers. Why the hell would it?

Instead of my talk being an inspirational nugget in their educational journey, all I managed to do was waste their time. I felt horrible. I had to go straight home and take a shower. When I told my wife what happened, she laughed it off saying, "It could not have been that bad." Oh, but it was...Nights like that make me understand why people fear public speaking more than death. I was the overweight, nerdy kid trapped on an island with the Lord of the Flies, and yet it had been totally preventable. What went wrong?

## KEY IDEA: SIMPLIFY YOUR MESSAGE

Whether you're speaking in front of a group of sophisticated and educated art lovers, giving a TED Talk, or ruminating in front of your friend's daughter's eighth-grade class, you need to simplify your message, because your audience is not going to do it for you. That was a lesson I learned too late to stop me from bombing in that classroom.

Communication is a two-way street, and you have only a finite amount of time to make your pitch. Attention is not an infinite commodity. You could be sharing the most important story of your life or trying to make the biggest deal you've ever made, but in the end, your audience's attention is going to wane. Suddenly, they'll be thinking about what they plan to prepare for dinner that night, the chores waiting for them at home, or the proposal that they need to finish up before tomorrow.

You are competing with all these things, most of which you have no idea about, so one of your goals needs to be respecting your audience's time. Simplifying your message is a surefire way to keep people's interest while you're telling your full story.

### KNOW WHO YOU ARE TALKING TO

I recently had an opportunity to interview several medical

professionals while doing work for one of our clients, the CHEST Foundation. They are the philanthropic arm of the American College of Chest Physicians, and their work is centered around championing lung health by supporting clinical research, community service, and patient education.

During one of their most recent annual conferences, I got to meet and interview physicians, nurse practitioners, and physicians' assistants about the differences in their ability to provide patient education. Regardless of their specialty or level of training and education, the story at the core of their professional existence aligned with the value of taking care of patients.

Working with this group, we noticed how difficult it can be for physicians to make the connection between the way they talk among themselves and the way they need to communicate with their patients and patients' caregivers. Ultimately, this disconnect can lead to worse outcomes for their patients, who, if intimidated by the scientific language, may not follow through with the treatments recommended to them. This language barrier can literally be the difference between life and death.

It was also important for the medical professionals to build trust with the patients and caregivers because when trust was established, they were more likely to receive accurate information about what was happening with the patient.

With trust, they got a much clearer sense of patients' diets, exercise habits, and whether they were smoking one pack of cigarettes a week or a pack a day.

Think about what your medical providers do when you go for a visit. They start by asking you a bunch of questions. Seek first to understand. Remember that from chapter two? It makes total sense. How do you know how to treat a patient if you don't have a complete picture of what is going on? How do you know if your product or service is right for your customer if you have no clue what their goals and grievances might be?

Yet patient education is a two-way street. It is vital for the patient and medical professional alike, since the professionals need to build trust in order to receive accurate information. Physicians particularly seem to struggle because they have far less time with each patient than the physicians' assistants or nurse practitioners. When you went to the doctor last, how long were you actually in front of your physician? Five minutes? Seven minutes at most? Given those constraints, think about how important it is for a physician not only to simplify their message but also speak in terms that you will actually be able to understand.

The same goes for other types of organizations, too. Think about how much time you have with your customer. Five to seven minutes is an eternity compared to a fifteen-to-thirty-second commercial or a ninety-second web video. So how much more important is it for you to be able to effectively simplify your message? Maybe it is not the difference between a person's life and death, but it could most certainly be the difference between life and death for your business or nonprofit.

## THE CURSE OF KNOWLEDGE

Simplifying your message can be a challenge because, chances are, you are very knowledgeable about what you do, but that knowledge can also be a curse.

It is exactly the same reason that I was unable to connect with my audience of soon-to-be- ninth-grade scholars. It is something called the "curse of knowledge." Experts like the respiratory clinicians are immersed in the minutiae of their profession. They have forgotten more about pulmonology and managing respiratory conditions than most of the population will ever know, by a factor of ten. If someone lives and breathes their company, profession, or project, then they never really stop. They inhale every aspect of it, every moment of every day. They are the expert in this thing they love, and they often feel compelled to perform an information dump every time they try to tell their story.

Sometimes, as the keeper of knowledge, we feel like we are going to explode if we don't share it. I can't watch any movie my fifteen-year-old has already seen without him saying, "This part is awesome," or "That guy is so funny," or "She is totally dead." He can't help it. He has the curse of knowledge. He can't prevent his spoiler Tourette's anymore than my wife or I can prevent yelling, "Shut up, Jonathan! Let us watch the movie."

Chances are, your customers are nicer people than we are as parents. They may not tell you to shut up, but they may tune you out. This is something you cannot afford because, like *8-Mile* Eminem, "you may only get one shot" to share your story. So **don't lose your audience** with your curse of knowledge.

In the end, you don't want to bombard the listener. Don't communicate every aspect of your passion, highlighting every problem it solves.

When this happens, all that's really accomplished is losing the audience. Recognize that your audience cannot possibly know your industry as well as you do. The most important thing you can do to ensure you are sharing your story effectively and engaging an audience, instead of driving it away, is to simplify your message. Drill it down to one key idea, if possible.

I often like to say that the videos we produce at Key Ideas are like trailers for the organizations and people we serve.

It isn't the full feature film, but it's going to get you excited to go see the whole thing. The trailer has highlights. It has music. It has drama. Most of all, it is going to set the stage and connect with people who see it in an emotional way, and they will be moved to action.

Overcoming the curse of knowledge is necessary to telling your story to the people who most need to hear it, because it helps you set up that unique selling proposition we mentioned earlier. And the best way to beat the curse is to simplify your way through it.

## HOW TO SIMPLIFY

There are a few main ways to go about making your story simple and effective. When we meet with a client, our first step is to seek first to understand by asking a lot of questions. Once we have a good handle on what their goals are, the industry that they are in, and to whom they would like to communicate, we develop what advertising and marketing professionals call the "creative brief."

Emphasis is on the brief and less on the creative. The entire document should be one page.

But don't let that brevity fool you. A creative brief is the foundation of any project, and it establishes, from the outset, what your goals, approach, and strategy are going to be.

This is an important document that will be the guide for your entire team as they move forward with a project.

Time can be the enemy of coherence and simplicity, and a brief like this can help you check yourself when, for example, it becomes June and you need to remember details of a story you might have conceived back in January. Memory is unreliable, and you might not have time to scour through pages and pages of notes in your Moleskine. A creative brief is a quick and easy way to make sure your goals are still being met. It will be readily available to anyone working on the project, even if they weren't a part of your initial creative meetings.

The creative brief is an important document, and while it can be good to have someone with an outside perspective work on it, it can certainly also be developed internally. Whatever route you choose, a solid creative brief will include seven main considerations:

## OVERVIEW

This is a paragraph about who you are and what you do. If you're simplifying the message of a company, this paragraph is mostly about the product you sell or the service you provide. It is not a doctoral thesis. It is just a high-level overview of what you do. You can include how long you have been around, but it does not need to include a list of all your accomplishments. We will get to that.

## PROJECT SCOPE

This is simply the task at hand. Is the project a twelve-page annual report, a PowerPoint presentation, or a fourth quarter advertising campaign? If it includes multiple projects under the same umbrella, you can list them all.

## WHO IS THE TARGET AUDIENCE?

Remember, it is important that you don't try to be everything to everyone. You must take the time to identify a target audience, and the more you consider your mission and niche, the more evident that audience will be. Identify your primary audience, then your secondary audience. Think of your primary audience as your bullseye and your secondary audience as the ring around it. By the end of this step, you'll have a handle on your primary audience, and the scope of your story will begin to take shape.

In a recent creative meeting with our client, City Year San Antonio, whose creative brief you'll find below, we identified our target audience as Generation Z (between eighteen and twenty-five years old). City Year deploys AmeriCorp members to serve as peer mentors for high-needs elementary school, middle school, and high school students. Their commitment is for eleven months, and many of these eighteen-to-twenty-five-year-olds move to a brand-new town. We quickly realized that our secondary audience needed to be the parents of those eighteen-to-twenty-five-year-olds since many of them are probably not yet completely independent. (I am about to turn forty, and I am still working on it!) Parents' influence on eighteen-to-twenty-five-year-olds can still be so strong that we could easily have swapped the target audience.

## WHAT MUST THE STORYTELLING DO?

This question should align with the outcomes you hope to experience. This is how you turn passives into promoters. In City Year's case, the goal was to build trust in and create awareness about the benefits of choosing City Year as a pathway to a career in education.

This section should also include a measurable outcome, like, "Receive 100 new applicants for ten positions that need to be filled by December," or "Increase sales leads by 10 percent over the next year." There are beautiful analytics that exist across multiple social media platforms that can help you measure your success. If it is working, don't stop, and don't change your message. Continue to build on the momentum you have created.

## WHAT MUST THE STORYTELLING SAY?

Don't overcomplicate this. You know what misconceptions you need to break and what aspects of your work should resonate most with your target audience. Remember, do not try to tackle too many issues with your storytelling. You will water down your message, and you will lose your audience. Beware of the curse of knowledge!

Synthesize your story into one key idea. In a creative brief for this book, my key idea would be, "There is glory in your story." One key idea is always going to be easier to simplify than a dozen smaller ones. That said, as part of your creative brief, you can also consider the secondary message. Do you have one? Does it enhance the key idea without distracting from it?

## WHAT ARE THE REASONS TO BE MOVED?

Think of this as your brag sheet. Imagine for a second that you are Donald Trump, and a camera is pointed at you. Only, make sure that what you are saying is true because people have this crazy way of finding out when you are lying. Call it strange, but your customers crave honesty and authenticity. This section can consist of bullet points. How long have you been around? What awards have you won? What is your impact, based on statistical data? What benefits do you offer that no one else does?

## WHAT IS THE TONE?

Finally, you want to determine the tone of your campaign. Think of this section as how you want people to feel. Excited? Inspired? Empathetic?

Choosing a tone may help inform your approach. Do you want your campaign to be comedic or serious? As far back as I can remember, GEICO insurance commercials have taken a very comedic and sometimes absurd tone. They have used cavemen, talking geckos, and sketches where bad things happen, but a reassuring final monologue proclaims, "However, there is good news! I just saved a bunch of money on my car insurance." What hasn't changed in all of these spots is the message that switching to GEICO will save you money on your car insurance. It works.

In contrast, USAA's commercials are serious and pull at the heart strings. There's no right or wrong way to go, because in the right hands, both approaches can be tremendously impactful. The tone that best suits your purpose will likely be determined by your culture and the brand you have established.

### A SAMPLE CREATIVE BRIEF

Ultimately, the creative brief exercise is a way to prioritize your thinking and to help simplify the story you want to tell. The brief is not made of concrete. It is a document that can change and evolve, but once you have it, you've created a guide for how you are going share your story, for the duration of whatever process or project you are working on.

Here is the actual creative brief that Key Ideas worked on

for City Year. It will show you just how brief—but also how targeted and necessary—this document can be.

## KEY (ID)EAS
MISSION-DRIVEN STORYTELLING

*City Year* CREATIVE BRIEF
STORYTELLING 2019

**OVERVIEW**

PROJECT SCOPE
- One 2-3 minute Recruitment video
- One 15-30 sec video for Social Media

WHAT MUST THE STORYTELLING DO?
Build trust and awareness of the benefits of choosing San Antonio as a place to live and start a career in education.

WHO IS THE TARGET AUDIENCE?
Generation Z (18-25 years old)
Parents of Generation Z (to build trust and awareness)

WHAT IS THE MOST IMPORTANT THING THE
STORYTELLING MUST SAY?
A year of service through City Year is a valuable investment and can be a life changing event.

WHAT ARE THE REASONS TO BE MOVED?
City Year offers a pathway to a career in education
San Antonio is rich with organizations focused on education
40% of corp members stay in the market, 25% stay in San Antonio.
City Year has been in San Antonio nearly 25 years
City Year will provide you with a network & relationships to advance your career
City year will help you develop a strong foundation:
Strong work ethic, resilience, productivity, financial management, clarity, community, $6,000 after graduation.
Ongoing professional development

WHAT IS THE TONE?
Inspirational / Educational

**MISSION-DRIVEN STORYTELLING**

A Sample Creative Brief from Key Ideas

## A LITTLE PREP GOES A LONG WAY

One of the biggest mistakes I made with my eighth-grade

presentation was my failure to rehearse. Winging it is never the best course of action. While it is important to remember the things you actually want to say, there are other considerations that go into a successful talk. Rehearsing your story and tailoring it to the audience will help you make those all-important emotional connections.

Remember: the most effective stories are those that connect with emotion, not rational thought. You may have given a presentation hundreds of times, but it is important to think through the ways that you are going to connect with that particular audience. You can't take a one-size-fits-all approach unless you want to risk standing in front of a room full of people with your proverbial pants around your ankles. It does not matter if it is an in-person presentation, an ad campaign, or a video that you are going to present at your next annual gala. As the saying goes, fail to plan, and you are just developing a plan to fail.

**SIMPLY SIMPLE**

Simplifying your message is not easy. It doesn't matter if your audience is a bunch of scary eighth graders or tech-savvy venture capitalists. The art of simplifying your message is vital to your success.

To end this chapter on simplifying your message, I'd like to share a simple sentiment: if you don't simplify your message, your audience simply won't care what you have to say.

Sketch Note Summary—Chapter 6

# CHAPTER SEVEN

# The Power of Positioning

In 2007, the globally managed hosting company, Rackspace, was rapidly growing, and its then-Chairman Graham Weston was looking to recruit new talent to San Antonio. Weston was an entrepreneur who had put down deep roots in San Antonio's business and philanthropic communities, and he was dedicated to bringing San Antonio's potential to the forefront. Rackspace had just acquired Webmail, a company whose founders had promised to make the move from Blacksburg, Virginia to San Antonio. That is, until the email.

The email was sent to Weston by one of Webmail's founders, who had changed his mind about coming to live in San Antonio. According to Bill's letter, the city didn't have enough venture capital to fund business startups, and the technology scene was dull, particularly compared to Austin, San Antonio's neighbor to the north.

Worse, there was not much of a desirable life outside of work. The downtown was almost absent, and the local bars and restaurants were unexciting. The city wasn't very walkable, and the founder even felt that there wasn't a convenient place to jog with his dog every morning. Basically, Bill claimed, San Antonio wasn't a place where entrepreneurship and tech could thrive.

How pessimistic of Bill to doubt that the top tech talent from around the world would not be crawling over themselves to hang out at Ripley's Believe It or Not, across from the Alamo and in between river barge cruises and overpriced margaritas. It's almost like he didn't know the movie *Selena* was filmed here in 1996.

Also, let's not dismiss the irony that the co-founder of Webmail would write his version of a "Dear John" letter via email.

Weston could have shrugged the email off. He could have gotten offended and written a nasty response. He could have mounted a defense of the city he loved, or he could have tried to bargain with the founder. Instead, he listened, and he let that email change his life.

That day, he forwarded the email to Julián Castro, who was then the mayor of San Antonio, and he said simply, "This is the city that we must build."

## THE TALE OF LONGO AND WESTON

Weston was clever enough to see that San Antonio was telling the wrong story about itself. The city had plenty of talent, but it wasn't readily apparent. San Antonio needed to rewrite its story so that young, tech-savvy, and startup-minded employees could see it as a great place to pursue their careers. The most important thing San Antonio had was its story, and that story was failing. At least, it was failing to communicate to anyone other than the tourists who were eager to visit the Alamo and the Riverwalk.

Around the time that Weston received the notorious email, his friend and former Rackspace customer, Nick Longo, was sitting in coffee shops trying to figure out his next move.

In 1996, Longo had created CoffeeCup Software, one of the first HTML editors, so that people could build their own websites. In just eleven years, it grew to a multimillion-dollar company with fifty million downloads and over twenty software programs. He also developed Bluedomino, a company to host the websites created on his software. To call it a success would be an understatement.

Nick was an unlikely tech success story because he accomplished all of this, not in NYC or Silicon Valley, but in a small city in the coastal bend of Texas called Corpus Christi. Nick once told me in an interview that he spent two years sleeping on the floor of the coffee shop he owned answering the customer service calls that would come in from all over the world. He was the owner and customer service department, and since his customers were in different time zones, he always had to be available.

Then, in 2007, Nick sold his companies, and suddenly he was like Taylor Swift without a complicated relationship to write about. Can you imagine where we'd be if Taylor Swift had fallen in love with her high school sweetheart, had three kids, and lived happily ever after? That's the kind of void Nick was living in.

Saddled with hefty non-compete agreements, he lacked a community where he could bounce around ideas. Nick thrives on ideating, and the isolation was slowly driving him bonkers. "No idea becomes real until it leaves your lips," Nick told me during an interview in early 2019. He desperately needed something to build and people to build it with.

Graham Weston and Nick Longo were an odd pairing. Weston is a soft-spoken leader who has a lineage connected to European aristocracy. Longo is a city slicker New Yorker who spent time in the military and who could have easily fit in as an NYPD beat cop. When you meet Nick, it is obvious that in both volume and in life he is living several decibels above the rest. If Longo were a comic book superhero his name would be…Nick Longo. If you ask me, that's already a great superhero name.

Thankfully, Weston and Longo found each other at just the right time. The duo teamed up for an epic US tour of coworking space in cities across the country to see what kinds of atmospheres these spaces fostered.

They noticed in almost every city that coworking spaces were innovative hot spots, and San Antonio was missing those kinds of vibrant workspaces or places for entrepreneurs to come together. On the plane back to Texas, Longo and Weston came up with the idea for a collaborative coworking space. Every week, members would dedicate one hour of their time to helping other members, or they could give a workshop once a month to share their expertise. It would be a community, in the true sense of the word—united by a common interest in ideas, creativity, and collaboration.

That's how Geekdom was born.

## GEEKDOM

In the Urban Dictionary, "geekdom" is the term for any place where more than two geeks gather. True to that name, the coworking space offered a central hub for business-minded dreamers. It was a place where entrepreneurs, programmers, and designers could explore ideas, conceive and grow businesses, and generally undertake the kind of intellectual and creative tinkering from which some of the best concepts arise.

Thanks to Weston and Longo's vision, Geekdom also became much more than that. It became an integral part of San Antonio's story. When Geekdom began in 2011, it occupied a single floor of one building downtown, but almost immediately, the growth took off. Suddenly, young companies wanted to move downtown; they wanted to be near other young companies. Web developers, entrepreneurs, and freelancers who had been operating out of coffee shops, home offices, and their mothers' basements all began to assemble like the Avengers.

Each new member introduced their network and unique skillsets to Geekdom, and it all took root in the center of the city. Folks that only drove downtown when their Aunt Bertha came to visit started walking around, eating at restaurants, and exploring parts of their city they never knew existed.

At the time, downtown San Antonio needed a new mission, and Geekdom helped provide it. The companies that set up shop in the Geekdom space helped start a new era for downtown and for the city as a whole. Now, seven years later, Geekdom has expanded to over 1,800 members, and it's had about $30 million's worth of economic impact on the city. The companies working out of Geekdom and those who have since outgrown the space collectively account for one of San Antonio's top twenty employers. Geekdom provided an ecosystem for new ideas, and it also spurred all kinds of related development throughout the city.

Today, San Antonio is much better suited to attract young tech talent and the like. There are places to walk, spots to jog with dogs, access to millions of dollars in venture capital funding, and most of all, places to create teams and pursue dreams. Companies are now choosing San Antonio as their home base, and one local college that once kept itself to the city periphery has invested seventy million dollars downtown to establish a school of data science and a National Security Collaboration Center.

Weston has called Geekdom members "the pioneers who are making San Antonio the city of its full potential," and that is certainly true. But that potential only became evident because Weston and Longo took that disgruntled email to heart. And instead of letting their egos take hold, they decided to change the story being told by and about the city they loved.

## HERO OR GUIDE?

The tale of Longo and Weston is an excellent case study that exemplifies all the characteristics of authentic storytelling that we have covered so far. In case you are one of those Quentin Tarantino types who likes to start a journey on chapter seven and work your way backwards, here is a recap:

- Seek first to understand. Weston and Longo flew across the country and asked questions of other startup communities and coworking spaces. They did not assume they had all the answers. They learned by talking to the experts. They tried to understand what was working and what wasn't, and then they asked themselves what would work within the community they wanted to serve.
- Be honest and authentic. They did not deny that problems existed. They were honest about the gaps that needed to be bridged in San Antonio. In fact, Weston sent Bill's email directly to the mayor. Why? Because transparency builds trust.
- First heart, then head. Weston's response to Bill's email was a heartfelt one. "This is the city we should build," he explained. He had conviction, and he had a vision. Weston spoke to people's hearts. He painted a picture of what the city could be.
- Be consistent. Weston and Longo did not try to be everything to everyone. They focused on tech and entrepreneurship. Instead of building a coworking space that would serve anyone looking for cheap office space,

they focused on creating a place where startups could be born. The general approach says, "This could be for me," while the specific approach says, "This is definitely for me." It's a subtle but meaningful difference. Know your audience and be consistent.

Geekdom—and the establishment of a tech scene in downtown San Antonio—has been successful for all of these reasons. But one thing that has contributed to that success, maybe more than all the other factors combined, is the way that Weston and Longo positioned Geekdom.

They didn't make it about them. Geekdom was, has, and always will be about the members.

Weston and Longo just invested in the ecosystem and attracted a community with diverse perspectives and skill-sets. It was a field of dreams for geeks, and the founders believed that if they made the space available, geeks would come.

Plus, Weston and Longo knew that, as experienced as they both were, they could never match the collective talent of the community. That's why every member was required to give back an hour a week. Of course, it didn't stop Weston and Longo from regularly mentoring—something they still do to this day—but they knew that their customers were the real heroes of San Antonio's story.

## THE POWER OF POSITIONING

It is vital as a storyteller to understand the power of positioning.

Donald Miller, the creator of StoryBrand, says that many organizations make the mistake of positioning themselves as the hero of the story, instead of focusing on their customers. Organizations go to great lengths to talk about how great they are and completely ignore the fact that their customers have a problem that they want to solve. Those customers often want to assume the role of hero in their own story, and sometimes, they just need a guide to get them there. That's where the organization should come in.

### KEY IDEA: BE THE GUIDE, NOT THE HERO

Miller developed his framework out of his experience as a screenwriter. In fact, if you start paying close attention, you can find this framework in your favorite movies and novels. (I caution you to keep it to yourself though. There is nothing worse than someone who taps their significant other during a movie and calls out the storytelling framework. At least, that's what my wife tells me after she elbows me in the ribs.)

Weston and Longo may not have known it, but the way they positioned Geekdom is the perfect example of Miller's framework:

1. There is a hero. Weston and Longo understood that the San Antonio tech and startup community was the actual hero of the story.
2. The hero has a problem. In this case, the problem was San Antonio's lack of a startup or tech scene.
3. Someone gives them a plan. Geekdom was the guide here. They didn't swoop in and take all the credit. They just offered the tech and startup community a way to move forward.
4. The plan calls the hero to action. Geekdom invited the community to share its ideas and to build something together.
5. The plan helps them avoid failure. Geekdom provided a space where the tech and startup community could come together and cultivate their network and skills.
6. The story ends in success. The companies that came out of Geekdom collectively make up the fourth largest employer in San Antonio, and their presence has completely transformed the downtown area.

It would have been a mistake to position Geekdom in any way aside from a place where a bunch of heroes get together to do hero shit. Geeky hero shit, but hero shit nonetheless. The members were the ones with a very diverse skillset, so they could learn from each other. The members were the ones developing solutions to real problems and building companies. The members were the ones hiring talent and adding members to the ecosystem.

Geekdom quickly became not only a place where startups were born but also a place where startups could fail. There were many successful startups that came out of the Geekdom community, but the ones that failed were often quickly scooped up by other startups. Why? Because when you are engaged in a battle to build your business, it helps to surround yourself with other people who have seen combat.

What was once two floors in an office tower is now an entire tech district in downtown San Antonio. San Antonio is not only recruiting tech talent but also entire tech companies who are expanding into the city. With over 1,700 employees, $100 million in capital raised across 300 launched startups, and over 1,250 new jobs, it is fair to say that San Antonio will never be the same. Weston and Longo positioned themselves as guides, and as a result, the work that they have started will most certainly outlive them.

Key Ideas was one of the original members of Geekdom when it started in 2011. We quickly grew as a result of the relationships I developed, and it was inspiring to be surrounded by a bunch of people way more talented than I was. I honestly don't know that Key Ideas would still be around as a company if it had not been for the relationships that I developed through Geekdom. I most certainly would not be writing this book.

I feel honored that I have an opportunity to be a guide to

help organizations maximize the impact they are having on the communities they serve. We get a ton of compliments on the work we do. The secret is that it is easy when you work with organizations that are making a true impact. They are indeed the true heroes.

## WHO WOULD YOU RATHER BE?

I challenge anyone reading this book to take a moment to truly be introspective. Is your goal to be a hero or to develop a sustainable business or nonprofit that truly makes a difference in people's lives?

The older I get, the more I realize that my success will never be defined by what I can accomplish. It will be defined by what I can help others accomplish. That is what guides do. That is what your customer is truly after. It is what Weston and Longo understood. It was what every great leader and storyteller throughout history understood.

Sketch Note Summary—Chapter 7

# CHAPTER EIGHT

# Transparency Builds Trust

E verything changes when you have kids. While shopping, it is easy to spot the couples who don't have kids because they are the ones who look rested and happy. My wife and I decided we had enough kids when McDonald's breakfast started costing us forty dollars. You are supposed to go to McDonald's to save money. I went through the drive-through, and when the cashier said, "Forty dollars," I turned to my wife, and I was like, "Did you order a mimosa? Since when do some biscuits with cheese add up to forty dollars? It is time to stop having kids! There are just too many of us!"

That year we also made a New Year's resolution to get healthier as a family. We started to limit our boys' portions, which was not a problem for our youngest son, Jonathan. He hardly ever wanted to eat much. We worried about him, but he was much cheaper to keep alive, so we tried to not make a big deal of it. Our oldest son Elijah was a different story.

It was tortellini night, Elijah's favorite. He finished his plate quickly, leaving us wondering if he had managed a breath between bites. He asked for seconds. Jen and I looked at each other, and without missing a beat, Jen said, "No. If you are still hungry, you can have some fruit or vegetables." Elijah shot me a look, hoping for a lifeline from his dad. He didn't get it. I said no, reinforcing that there were healthier options if he was truly still hungry. He cut me with a cold stare, and when I would not compromise, he proceeded to use a tactic mastered and passed down from the Maestas's tribe for generations: The Silent Temper Tantrum.

The STT is even worse than a temper tantrum because not only does it attack your emotions, it aims to destroy your mind. Elijah would not engage for the rest of the night. How could he? His body was too frail from starvation to find words.

Naturally, I got frustrated because this transpired while Jen and I had friends over. I put him on a time-out, which made the tantrum no longer subtle or silent. I raised my voice and said, "You are going to sit in here so you can think about exactly what you did wrong." Some time passed, and I finally went into the room to collect the apology that by this time would, of course, be very well thought out.

I turned to him and said, "Okay, buddy, what do you have to say for yourself?"

He looked up at me, wiping tears from his magnified brown eyes and said, "I am sorry."

"Okay, what are you sorry for?"

"I am sorry that I was upset because YOU DID NOT GIVE ME ENOUGH TO EAT."

Say what???

It was like he had figured out how to channel some mystical council of Maestas STT masters that had given him a final nuclear Pokémon to play. I might have respected the response had I not been the victim of it. I slammed the door and marched back to find my parenting partner to tell her what Elijah had just said.

When I told Jennifer, I fully expected her to be just as upset with him as I was. Instead, she turned to me in a way only a wife with a prophetic whisper can, and she said, "He is just like you!" Right before letting out a large laugh.

I replied, "I know, right? Wait...what? What do you mean? How did this become about me?"

She said, "When you get mad, you shut down, and you have a really hard time apologizing."

So I did what all good Christian husbands do. I got mad and refused to talk to her for the rest of the night. I lamented that my refusal to give my son seconds had somehow turned into a lesson about how I handle conflict. I should have just let him eat the damn noodles!

Upon reflection, I realized that I was judging Elijah for something I do myself. I also recognized two major things. First, I have some work to do when it comes to conflict resolution. Second, it is so valuable to have someone in my life who is willing to be transparent with me, even when it is something I may not want to hear. A true partner does not tell you what you want to hear. They tell you what you need to hear. If we focus only on self-preservation, we will never reach our fullest potential.

Jennifer is the person I trust most in the world mostly because she has never failed to be transparent with me. Mistrust comes from a lack of transparency, or at least a perceived lack of transparency. You can't hope to move people through storytelling if there is no trust. The last Key Idea is also one of our core values.

### THE MOST IMPORTANT TRAIT

It is hard to overstate the importance of transparency for storytelling. Not just as a storytelling principle but as a way to live.

Author Gay Hendricks once wrote, "A successful life is an authentic life. Happiness and creativity rest on a foundation of transparency to yourself and others. Knowing your own heart and speaking clearly to others keep you on the path." Everything that we've talked about in this book so far starts with being honest with yourself and your audience.

Honesty and, when appropriate, vulnerability will help you connect with your audience. Remember, there is glory in your story.

### TRANSPARENCY PAYS OFF

The best way to overcome a mistake or a shortcoming is to be open about it. Transparency gives you the power to shape your story. Without it, you leave your narrative open to being hijacked or misconstrued. Either way, opacity hurts your story.

Transparency also does the heavy lifting of building trust

with your audience. Owning up to mistakes, whether you're a political candidate or a company, will have tangible results in the long run. Southwest Airlines even coined the phrase "Transfarency," showing how important that trait is to their customers. It showcases a philosophy in which customers are treated honestly and fairly, and low fares actually stay low. No unexpected bag fees, change fees, or hidden fees. It is no surprise that Southwest Airlines has been profitable forty-five years in a row. It goes beyond cost. It is cultivated in their culture.

A project we worked on with one of our partners, San Antonio Water Systems (SAWS), is another example of how transparency builds trust in storytelling. Water is our most precious commodity, and in the past, SAWS wasn't always the best steward of this resource. Now, SAWS has won awards for sustainability.

Imagine turning on your local news, to any affiliate, and getting a daily report about how high or low your aquifer levels are. Or getting a water bill and being able to see how much water you are using compared to your neighbors. If this seems odd, it might be because you live somewhere other than San Antonio, Texas.

SAWS has created a citywide culture of conservation and generated awareness for a resource that most parts of the world aren't fortunate enough to take for granted. With over a million people expected to move to San Antonio in the next twenty years, it is imperative to continue to diversify the community's water resources.

When SAWS approached Key Ideas about telling the story of their newest brackish water recycling plant, we had a lot of questions. First of all, what the hell is a brackish water desalination plant?

Well, brackish water is a mixture of fresh and saltwater. By desalinating the water in the Wilcox Aquifer, SAWS was able to reduce San Antonio's dependence on its drought-sensitive primary Aquifer. Once the water is treated, the Wilcox Aquifer can provide twelve million gallons of drinking water every day. This is enough to supply drinking water to 53,000 households. It was a previously untapped resource that took more than ten years to come to fruition.

Water has always been vital to the growth of San Antonio. The city developed around the San Antonio River, and as the city grew, so did the need to diversify its water sources. The new SAWS plant and its sustainability initiatives meant more water diversification for the seventh largest city in the country.

SAWS wanted to tell the story of the plant, but to their credit, they did not want a technical video voiced over by engineers talking about the process of recycling brackish water. They wanted to tell a story about the importance of a resource that is taken for granted in developed countries.

Greg Wukash, the Education Director of SAWS, used a remarkable quote in one of his presentations: "To say that we take water for granted is, in some ways, to give us too much credit. We don't take water for granted, because we don't notice it enough to take it for granted" (Charles Fishman, *The Big Thirst*). Fishman and Wukash are right. We turn the faucet on, and water is just there. We flush the toilet, and we don't think twice about the potential consequence that action could have on our drinking water supply. This is a luxury not afforded to my friends in Liberia, Africa who just happened to be born on the other side of the Atlantic Ocean.

In Liberia, a deadly series of civil wars decimated the country's infrastructure. Millions of people were left without access to clean water. The country installed some water wells, but they are insufficient. There are up to thousands of families dependent on a single well, and people have to walk miles just to get access to water. The lack of water has significant social side effects, heightening conflicts between neighboring groups of people who needed the precious resource. Other water sources available in some areas are often used as animal drinking spots, laundry facilities, and latrines, meaning that those scarce supplies of water are often tainted. Organizations like Liberia Now are trying to address the country's water needs, but on a daily basis, Liberians are reminded of just how precious clean water is.

These issues deserve more attention, so the opportunity of sharing the importance of water and sustainability got our entire team fired up. It would prove to be one of the most challenging projects we would take on. That might seem odd, since SAWS had plenty of projects to talk about. Making the case that we all take water for granted and need to focus more on sustainability wasn't the hard part. What made it such a challenge was telling an authentic story about what inspired SAWS to pursue this path. SAWS's sustainability efforts weren't driven by an epiphany in their leadership. They were driven by a lawsuit filed against the City of San Antonio and SAWS by the Sierra Club.[13]

SAWS used to be split into three systems: the Waste Water Department, City Water Board, and Reuse District. Each of these utilities was overpumping water from what was, at that time, San Antonio's only water source, the Edwards Aquifer. Edwards is home to several endangered species, including the Fountain Darter, Riffle Beetle, and a blind salamander that, when fully grown, reaches a whopping thirteen centimeters. In the early 1990s, heavy pumping by the three major utilities was putting these species in danger of extinction.

---

13 If you would like to watch the video, you can see it here: https://vimeo.com/250187473.

The City of San Antonio and then-mayor Nelson Wolff had a very difficult choice to make. They could forge ahead and fight the lawsuit, or they could take what would ultimately be a much harder path: to admit fault and address the issue.

Russell Johnson, a Water Rights Attorney involved in the process, said, "San Antonio was severely crippled, even with the threat to its water supply, much less an actual restriction on our ability to actually use that water." He continued, "We had to fundamentally change the law in order to protect our water supply. It wasn't going to be easy to do that; it certainly wasn't going to be cheap, but by doing so, we could ensure that our community had a protected and reliable water supply, not just for then but for the future. It is something we should not just be proud of but that we should fight to protect."

Nelson Wolff made the decision to pull all the water utilities under one department and create San Antonio Water Systems.

It was ironic that a blind five-inch salamander we never see would have such a tremendous impact on a natural resource we never think about. Ultimately the decision to make the huge investment in San Antonio's water has led to diversifying San Antonio's water supply to eight sources, in addition to the Edwards Aquifer. San Antonio also has a huge water recycling program that takes the stuff we flush and turns it into the water used in car washes, public park irrigation, plant cooling, and beautification projects. (That recycled water is actually clean enough to drink, but the community would probably never get past its humble beginnings.)

SAWS knew they had a great story to tell, but it would be disingenuous to do so without admitting to the bumps along the way. We could have easily omitted the lawsuit, but imagine what would have happened if someone other than SAWS brought that part of the story to light.

Fortunately, SAWS chose the path of transparency.

SAWS was committed to addressing its failures in the past, particularly the Sierra Club lawsuit, and sharing how those lessons shaped and formed the ways in which SAWS developed. SAWS' leaders knew they had to tell that story in order to build trust with the public and reinforce their commitment to investing in projects that contribute to San Antonio's sustainability. They knew it wouldn't be enough to simply talk about the data or the science behind what they were doing.

Rather than circle around the lawsuit and other previous problems, they owned up to all of it. In the end, this transparency helped shape the conversation. Transparency changes the dynamic in any discussion, and by owning the parts of your story that aren't so flattering, you can keep your story focused on where you want to go, not necessarily where you've been.

SAWS has been recognized nationally as the model for sustainability and how to diversity water sources. For anyone interested, the Texas blind salamander is still listed as vulnerable on the endangered species list, but the population is stable. In 2013, the US Fish and Wildlife Service approved a Habitat Conversation Plan that will minimize stress on endangered species, including the Texas blind salamander.

## LEAD WITH THE BAD NEWS

Boxers call it "leading with your chin," and it's usually a recipe for disaster, at least if you're trying to make a living as a pugilist. If you're a storyteller though, it's a good idea. Leading with the unflattering or negative angle to your story, admitting your faults, and revealing where you have fallen short in the past are great ways to show your willingness to give a complete accounting of how you got here. It establishes you as someone willing to be open and honest about yourself, warts and all. Your audience will appreciate that.

Popular radio host, author, and entrepreneur, Dave Ramsey, has built an empire giving regular people like you and me advice on how to get out of debt and build wealth. His presentations are entertaining and practical, and they embody every characteristic of authentic storytelling we have talked about in this book.

One of the things I admire most is that he does not hide the hard parts of his story, even if they could potentially damage his credibility. For example, the introduction to his money management class ends with a discussion of how difficult it was for him and his wife to go through bankruptcy. How many financial advisors do you know who lead with, "I know what you are feeling right now. I had to file for bankruptcy once?"

This transparency highlights the authenticity of his story and goes a long way to humanize it. It sets up a paradigm where peoples' trust grows as Ramsey's willingness to be open and honest becomes his defining trait.

## CRISIS MANAGEMENT

The show *The West Wing* ran on NBC for seven years, beginning in 1999. If you don't remember, the incredibly popular show focused on the goings-on within the West Wing of the White House. While Martin Sheen portrayed President Jed Bartlett for the show's entire run, the final season ended with the election of Rep. Matt Santos (played by Jimmy Smits) to the Presidency.

One episode offered an incredibly valuable lesson in transparency that works as well in the real world as it did in the fictional one.

In this episode, Santos was in the heat of his campaign against Republican challenger, California Senator Arnold Vinick, portrayed by Alan Alda. On television, as in reality, California is an important state for any presidential candidate to carry, so when an accident in a nuclear power plant in his home state turned fatal, the pro-nuclear power Vinick was in a tough spot.

His advisors suggested skirting the issue and avoided tackling it head-on. They saw little benefit, and in a piece of wrong-headed thinking, they believed addressing the issue would prolong its taint on his campaign.

Vinick refused to listen, and in a move reminiscent of the smartest crisis managers in the world, he pivoted and faced the crisis head-on. In the episode, Vinick held a press conference and didn't shy away from the crisis, remaining at the podium until every reporter had their questions answered. It was a character study of a seasoned politician making a seasoned politician move.

The message of the episode, which also applies to the real world, is that by confronting the issue, Alda's character limited the amount of time the story dominated headlines, or at least his own tangential role in the story. He also did not let his silence on the issue allow the media to fill in the gaps.

## TAKING OUR OWN MEDICINE

Early on in our firm's existence, we missed a deadline. We'd promised something to a client by a certain date, and we didn't quite hit it. As a young company, it might have been tempting to run away from our mistake or to try and smooth things over with the client by deflecting blame for our failure. Instead, our path was clear.

First, we issued the client a refund check for the entire amount they'd paid us. That was a good start, but it still lacked the humanity that comes with transparency. In addition to the refund, we apologized to our client in person, in their offices, with us an offering of fruit cups in tow.

The gestures did not go unappreciated. First, and most importantly, they forgave us for our mistake. Additionally, since we'd delivered the work we had promised and they were able to make full use of it, the client refused to take our check. Not only that, but they were so happy with our work *and* our openness about the missed deadline that they became our second-biggest client that year and remain a client to this day. Our transparency built trust at a time we were still establishing our working relationship.

## TRANSCENDING FAILURE

One underappreciated aspect of transparency is its curative power over failure. To be clear, I think failure is an important waypoint on the path to success. The trick is not to get mired in it. Failure is only helpful if it is ultimately one of the factors in your success, rather than a prolonged state of being.

In the beginning, it's going to be hard. Being transparent about the things you've failed at, the marks you've missed, and the things that did not go exactly as planned is a difficult practice to start. Over time, though, an amazing alchemy takes place. The more open you are about your failures when you tell your story, the more the walls seem to collapse. It doesn't mean that the pain or sting of those failures go away. Certain stories may always be hard to tell. But the more you talk about them, the more you make those struggles part of the story you tell about yourself. Then your story will do more and better work for you, and it will bring even more help to those who hear it.

It has been almost twelve years since my divorce, but I still talk about it. I know my transparency and vulnerability about how I got to where I am now opens audiences up in a way that I couldn't reach if I kept that part of my life a secret. Transparency has worked for me, and when applied appropriately, it has worked with our clients. In fact, the story we produced for SAWS was nominated for an Emmy in Texas.

We think Mr. Rogers would be proud of our ability to build

trust through transparency. He was a master at it. Because of that, there are generations of kids who not only are more educated thanks to his help but who are much better neighbors too.

Sketch Note Summary—Chapter 8

CHAPTER NINE

# Start Something You Can't Finish

A few years back Jennifer and I traveled to Barcelona, Spain, where we had an opportunity to tour the Basílica La Sagrada Família. La Sagrada Família is a Roman Catholic basilica and the most visited monument in Spain. It is widely believed to be the best interpretation of Gothic architecture since the Middle Ages. I had visited once before, but I didn't actually go in. To be honest, I thought it looked a little busy. Kind of showy, like the coworker who wears way too much jewelry and likes to talk with his hands. I now know that I didn't fully appreciate it because I didn't seek first to understand the story behind the Sagrada Família. On my return visit, I was armed with a better concept of the church's construction and the story *behind* the building.

La Sagrada Família is one of seven UNESCO World Heritage sites created by famed Catalan architect Antoni Gaudí. Gaudí was a very religious man, and he was nicknamed "God's Architect" because of his sources of inspiration and his use of religious imagery. Gaudí used to famously say, "Originality is returning to the origin." For Gaudí, this meant drawing inspiration from creation. He needed to look no further than the world around him to be moved.

When you're inside the basilica, the columns supporting the spires resemble tree trunks. They begin wide at the base and narrow down as they rise, like the branches of a tree would. You can find architectural elements that look like honeycombs, and animal-shaped gargoyles strategically dotting the exterior. There are parts that look as if you have entered a cavern, composed of spiral staircases and conoid-shaped roofs. The roof Gaudí designed for the architectural school located on the Sagrada Família's grounds resembles a magnolia leaf. The undulating shape, reminiscent of the blade of a leaf, channels rainwater that can be recaptured, creating a sustainable architectural design feature taken straight from nature.

Every element within the building has a story to tell, and the entire structure is a work of art. I will never forget standing inside and gazing up into the light filtering through these magnificent stained glass windows, throwing out colors I'd never quite seen before. If I had this entire book to describe how spectacular La Sagrada Família is, I would not even come close. Simply put, it is a marvel.

The detail that I find the most inspiring about this building is the fact that it is still being built. Construction started in 1882 and it won't be complete until the year 2026, 144 years after construction began.

La Sagrada Família Under Construction, 1905

Think about that for a moment.

That means that a group of people, including Gaudí (who died in 1926), started this project knowing they would never live to see it finished. They did it anyway. They made the plans, shared the vision, raised the money, assembled the teams, and even kept going after encountering some monumental obstacles. From the moment it began, the construction of La Sagrada Família was a multigenerational proposition, and it has continued because it's about something much bigger than any single person who has ever been involved. Even Gaudí, its architect.

I like to think that it was never about the building, no matter how marvelous it actually is. Instead, it's about what it might inspire in the people who visit the building year after year, generation after generation. Gaudí recognized how important it was to start something he couldn't finish.

## KEY IDEA: START SOMETHING YOU CAN'T FINISH

Starting something you can't finish requires you to commit to something bigger than yourself. It's in direct opposition to the things we are told when we're young. Growing up, you undoubtedly heard your parents say, "If you start something, you better finish it." We are warned not to join the team unless we can commit to being at all the games and practices. We are not going to get the dog unless we're willing to walk, feed, and clean up after it.

When I say that you should start something you can't finish, I am not talking about mowing the lawn, cleaning your house, or going to college. Those are things that you can and should finish. I am talking about dedicating your life, or at least a piece of your life, to a higher purpose.

Chapters one through eight have focused on how you can move an audience through a powerful story. Starting something you can't finish is about living a better story. I once heard author and pastor, Craig Groeschel, say, "If we are not dead, we are not done." This applies to all of us, no matter how old, stressed, or hurt we may be.

Many people reading this book may already have chosen to live a life of service. Maybe you have served in the military or are married to someone who has. Maybe you work in schools, hospitals, churches, or other mission-driven organizations. Maybe you have reorganized your personal or business finances to facilitate a higher purpose. If so, you have already started something you can't finish.

I don't think you can realize your fullest potential as a human being without having a goal bigger than yourself. Without it, I am certain that you won't reach your full potential as a storyteller. Authentic, creative, and transparent storytelling that uses emotion to connect with audiences and inspire action is most effective when it helps your audience connect to a higher aspiration. You want people to be inspired to undertake something they might think is unattainable.

Gaudí, and presumably the subsequent stewards of his vision for La Sagrada Família, hoped not only to honor God through the work but to also provide an environment where generations of patrons could come to know and worship Him. By committing himself to the service of something bigger than himself, Gaudí, in a way, almost became immortal. Today, he is heralded as one of the most famous architects in history.

Gaudí would likely have been famous in his time even if he'd declined the offer to take on La Sagrada Família, but his fame and influence would have been limited to experts in architecture or to his nineteenth-century Spanish contemporaries. By connecting his story to a higher mission—by starting a story he could not finish—Gaudí remains an important cultural influence to this day.

## FINDING YOUR WHY

My life's honor is helping tell the stories of organizations who do some of the most meaningful work in the world. Every one of these organizations is living out the idea of starting a story they can't finish, a story that's too big to be contained within a single life. That's something all of us can do. If you are reading this book, there's a great chance you already are.

The idea of starting something you can't finish is simple

enough to understand. However, as we continue this work together, there are a few things we shouldn't forget:

## I. RESTORATION IS POSSIBLE

In the Old Testament of the Bible, there is a story about a man named Ezra. He was a priest, scribe, and a great leader. So great, in fact, that his name even means "help." At the end of the seventh century B.C.E., the Babylonian King Nebuchadnezzar destroyed Jerusalem and carried the Jewish people away as slaves. They lived in captivity for years, exiled from their home, forced to work for a king who treated them poorly. Ezra was among these captives.

Decades later, in 539 B.C.E., Babylon was overthrown by the Persian King Cyrus. Cyrus granted freedom to the original twelve tribes of Israel, but only two of the tribes went back to rebuild. Ezra was among them. When they arrived, they found a devastated, unfamiliar land.

Let's try to get a little context. I want you to think about a time where, maybe you weren't captive, but you were delayed. Maybe you had to spend extra hours in an airport, or maybe your flight got canceled. Now, imagine that when you were finally able to leave the airport, you headed home, only to find out that the airline had destroyed your house. How upset would you be? Multiply that by 10,000. That would have been the vibe that these people were feeling at the time.

People's spirits must have been broken. What differentiated Ezra was that he didn't give in to despair. He remained faithful. In Ezra 9:8, he says, "Now for a short time, O Lord our God, you have been gracious to us and have let some of us escape from slavery and live in safety in this holy place. You have let us escape from slavery and have given us new life."

He didn't focus on the destruction. He focused on the potential. They had the chance to restore their homes and lead new lives. Ezra wasn't just referring to the restoration of a place. He was referring to a restoration of the spiritual passion of God's people.

Maybe you believe in God, or maybe you just believe in people. Either way, Ezra teaches us a powerful lesson: if you want to start something you can't finish, you must first believe that restoration is possible. You have to know that the power to develop is as much with you as it is with the people you serve.

You may not be experiencing physical slavery, like the people in the Babylonian exile did, but resentment, grief, loss, and depression have the power to prevent us from living the kind of lives we were meant to live. Often, people in positions of influence have to be reminded of this, especially when they find themselves in a season of brokenness. Even if you've seen restoration happen time and time again among the people your organization has served, you have to remember that restoration is also possible for you.

## 2. RESTORATION IS HARD

Restoration is hard. Even when you are doing the right thing, that doesn't mean that it will be easy. Telling your story can be hard because, by definition, taking on something bigger than yourself is hard.

Nehemiah 4:17 says, "Those who carried materials did their work with one hand and held a weapon with the other."

When Ezra started to rebuild that devastated land, you can be sure that he hit some obstacles. Workers encountered the physical obstacles of building walls and carrying stones. Community members had to defend their new land, protecting the vulnerable from more powerful communities that might try to attack in a time of weakness. Leaders carried the less tangible burdens of guiding people through harsh times. Ezra saw that restoration was possible, but it took immense resolve to work toward that possibility.

Building La Sagrada Família has also been hard. They have had delays and problems, including running out of money.

In 1926, Gaudí was coming from the construction site and was hit by a tram on his way to a different church. He died three days later, at the age of seventy-three, after succumbing to his injuries. At the time of Gaudí's death, La Sagrada Família had three quarters remaining to complete.

Architects have come and gone. In fact, the first designer of La Sagrada Família wasn't Gaudí; it was a man named Francisco de Paula del Villar, but he resigned due to design disputes.

In the 1930s, construction was interrupted during the Spanish Civil War, when anarchists broke into the basilica's workshop and damaged the plans and plaster casts Gaudí had left behind. It took sixteen years to get back on track.

Obstacles abounded. And yet the story of the basilica continued.

Being part of something bigger than yourself is always going to draw resistance. Sometimes the resistance comes from people or forces that don't want you to succeed, and sometimes we are our own worst enemy. Regardless, being part of something bigger than yourself is hard precisely because it is worth it. There are parts of our world that are dark, but not even darkness can overcome the light.

## 3. RESTORATION IS CONTAGIOUS

Our church is located in one of San Antonio's most famous theaters, the Cameo Theater. It began as the first African American theater in the city, and it hosted a roster of famous blues musicians, including B.B. King. In later life, other acts like Metallica took to the Cameo's stage.

Eventually, the theater shut down and suffered from neglect and disuse. The building became dilapidated. At some point, electrical codes became more of a suggestion than actual protocol. I ran a youth ministry in the café connected to the theatre. Middle school and high school students learned about Jesus surrounded by air redolent of a Porta-Potty. It was not a pleasant place, but the students never once complained.

My church eventually bought the building and got down to the process of resurrecting the once-amazing structure. From the beginning, though, the restoration of the Cameo had less to do with the building itself, and everything to do with what would happen inside it. In other words, the building was not *about* the building. It was about the work that was going to happen in the building. It was about the work that was going to happen in peoples' lives because they had a church to call home. The restoration wasn't about the beauty of an artistic building. Its purpose was to serve the people who came through its doors.

I have had an opportunity to serve in multiple ways at this church: as a youth pastor, a weekend producer, and as the communicator who would deliver the weekend message. I have done this for years. I can't tell you how moving it is to know that the work always matters to someone. Weekend after weekend you can look around and see people that are at various stages of life. Some of them in celebratory seasons, while others are in seasons of deep grief. It has always been inspiring to serve with people who show up and give their best every weekend because of what God was capable of doing for the people who came to the Cameo.

We often heard stories about the impact that the church had on people's lives, but there were just as many stories that we never heard, and surely some that we never will. I hope that this book has made an impact on you, but my greater hope is that it makes an impact on the people you serve, people that I will never have an opportunity to meet. Teaching others how to share their stories is, for me, a process of starting something I can't finish.

Almost three decades ago, fifty people formed the church, and they used to meet in a high school cafeteria. Of course, they hoped to have an impact, but there is no way they could fully understand what would become of their efforts. The church eventually grew to over 5,000 regular attendees, and it planted two additional churches, including the one that restored the Cameo Theater. Thousands of people have been baptized, and millions of dollars have been invested in social action ministries, both locally and abroad. The church built a Pre-K-12 school in Liberia, Africa and supported an orphanage in Chihuahua, Mexico. They offered transitional living programs and summer camps to students at risk of being sex trafficked in Moldova. Their efforts have helped keep families together who were at risk of separation because they were experiencing homelessness. They've collected millions of pounds of food for the local food bank.

I have personally met and interviewed people who have overcome some of the hardest circumstances imaginable. A woman who found love and was able to start a family after years of living on the streets, in and out of jail for prostitution and drug-related charges. Couples whose marriages have been saved. A friend, now a dad of three, who was prepared to take his own life after years of alcohol addiction. Those beautiful children would not exist if there hadn't been someone who picked up the phone and prayed with him when he called. The light of those original fiftymembers, even those who've left this earth, continues to shine through everyone who has been touched. Still, there is so much work left to be done.

I know that restoration is contagious because I was once a very bitter and totally broken man. Somehow, I found my way to a church full of perfectly imperfect people. Had it not been for the fifty people who started the church, most of whom I never met, I don't think I would be here today. My beautiful, fearless five-year-old might not be bending us over in laughter with her impeccable comedic timing. I might not have experienced the joy of seeing my two sons grow into strong and incredibly talented men.

And to think there was once a time in my life where I honestly felt I would never love again. How wrong I was.

I am so grateful that these people understood that restoration was possible. At the end of the day they understood that they were building something so much bigger than themselves. A building is like a temple—the building may serve as the physical space to meet, but the real temple is the people who walk through its doors and who make themselves available to others.

Even if you don't believe in God, the example of the Cameo shows just how powerful and contagious restoration can be. We all have the opportunity to use our stories to impact other peoples' lives. You never know when you might just be the difference for someone.

Telling the story only you can tell is an act of restoration. You're restoring yourself, especially if you allow yourself to do all the things that we've talked about in this book.

## WE ALL HAVE A ROLE TO PLAY

It is easy to focus on major figures in world history who have given themselves wholly in the service of something bigger than them. Martin Luther King, Jr., Abraham Lincoln, or more recently, Malala, are great examples. These are all amazing people, but we may find it hard to see ourselves in the same category. You might be saying, "Slow down. I want to make a difference, but I am not trying to die for it. Can't I just become a reading buddy or something?" You totally can. We may admire Superman, but we often see ourselves as his meek alter ego, Clark Kent.

Most of us do not see ourselves leading a revolution, and that is understandable. Neither do I. I have too many shows on Netflix to watch. What I want to suggest is, no matter our place in society, we have a role to play. Even if it's not as grandiose as the Sagrada Família, we all have things we can start without finishing.

If you met my grandmother, you'd understand.

She was born in Monterrey, Mexico and became a US citizen in her late seventies. This, in itself, was impressive: she undertook learning US history and passing the citizenship exam at such an advanced age.

She died in 2018 at age ninety-nine.

Soft-spoken and kind, she lived purely in service to others. In my memory, she was always cooking for us or asking if there was anything she could do for me, my sister, or my mom. I grew up in Sacramento, California, and when grandma would visit, she never seemed to sit down. Her joy was in washing clothes or cooking dinner, and as much as we tried to tell her to relax and enjoy the vacation, she wouldn't.

I admired her for the way she handled loss. Her husband died when she was twenty-two, leaving her to raise three young children alone. She never remarried and instead dedicated the next three decades to ensuring her children had everything they needed. I was always fascinated by that aspect; widowed at twenty-two, she never took off her wedding ring. She was loyal. In fact, on one of our last Thanksgivings together, she came to my in-laws' house. My father-in-law reached over to give her a kiss on the cheek, and she slapped him. It was hilarious. It was totally innocent on my father-in-law's part, but my grandma was not afraid to slap a dude in his own house on Thanksgiving.

In the Bible, Jesus recognized the might of the widow:

> As Jesus looked up, he saw the rich putting their gifts into the temple treasury. He also saw a poor widow put in two small coins. 'I tell you, this poor widow has put in more than all the others. All these other people gave from their wealth, but she, out of poverty, put in all she had to live on.' (Luke 21: 1-4)

That is a perfect reflection of my grandmother. She was not wealthy, but she gave everything she had to the people she loved.

For some of us, our story is everything we have to give. Know that it is more than enough.

We all have the opportunity to be for other people the person that my grandmother was for the people she loved. We are surrounded by people who can benefit from our story, whether it's family, friends, or coworkers. For something to be bigger than yourself, it doesn't have to change the fate of nations or undo decades of history. It just has to be drawn from an authentic, unique place. It has to be a story only you can tell.

That was the first Key Idea I gave you: there is glory in your story. And I truly mean it. Your story is unique and valuable. In fact, it's the most valuable thing that you own.

That's because storytelling is the most powerful force in the world. It can guide and instruct. It can get you what you want and provide what you need. It can move whole societies, or, more humbly but no less importantly, it can help the hurting coworker down the hall. At its best, storytelling can connect you to something bigger than yourself. It can have an impact on people you've never met, for generations to come.

We're on this earth for a short time; how great would it be to use that time in service to something that will outlast us?

Share your stories and share them often.

When you are doing great work—when you are starting things you can't finish—you will never have a shortage of stories to tell.

Sketch Note Summary—Chapter 9

# Next Steps

I f you're still feeling stuck, here's an exercise that can help you identify your unique story. Before you can move anyone else, you have to have a great narrative leavened with a healthy dose of authenticity.

No matter what the situation is, the person listening to your story will want to know your motivation. Get used to it. That question never really goes away: *Why are you so passionate about this work? Why do you want to come here for school? What's your deal, anyway?*

The quality of your answer is going to be important.

To help thoughtfully craft your response, map out the important milestones in your life to this point. Begin by writing down your birth year at one end of a line, and then write down the current year at the other end. In between, mark milestones along the way—both the highs and the lows. Then, think of the most vivid memories at each milestone.

Over time, you'll find yourself charting out the parts of your stories that explain who you are, what you want, and how you would like to live. Then, you begin harnessing the power of your most powerful tool—the story you tell about yourself—and are actively mapping the contours long before you are ever asked to share it.

Take the Next Step

# Acknowledgments

I have said many times that the reason I started doing stand-up was because it was cheaper than therapy. On my best nights the audience would trade me a little self-esteem through laughter in exchange for my stories. Although I am grateful for these exchanges, they only lasted for twenty or thirty minutes, and in most cases alcohol was involved. Ted Flanagan and Carolyn Purnell from Scribe spent collectively a year and a half listening to me rant in increments of an hour. As far as I can tell they did it completely sober. Ted, in addition to asking thoughtful questions, thank you for your positivity and for organizing what must have felt like a series of disconnected stories. I thoroughly enjoyed our conversations. You will forever be my main man in Massachusetts. Carolyn Purnell, you stepped in at a time where I felt stuck. You quickly lent a fresh perspective and helped me to get to the finish line. Thanks for laughing at my dad jokes, for constantly encouraging me, and for the intimate relationship you formed with my grammar.

To my publishing managers Kayla Sokol and Libby Allen. Thank you for being great guides of my first literary journey. You never made me feel guilty for checking out when I got busy at work. Your timely reminders that I had a book to finish helped me stay on track.

To Lorenzo Gomez for being one of Key Ideas' biggest promoters. When I met you, Key Ideas had been around for ten years. Your invitation to be a part of the Geekdom ecosystem made me feel like a startup again. Thank you for continuing to invest in me and Key Ideas. The opportunity to write this book is truly a dream come true. Jennifer and I are proud to be your friends and a part of the Geekdom Media family.

To Key Ideas' storysmiths Christopher Branca and Stephanie Gaitan. Thank you for being patient with me as I worked on this book for the last eighteen months. I can't thank you enough for sticking with me through some very difficult years. You make it easy to come to work every day, and your talent and passion for our work is a constant source of inspiration. You are the hands and feet that make each story we tell meaningful and memorable.

I have to thank every client who has helped me live my

dream for the past eighteen years. It is easy to share powerful stories when the organizations you partner with are doing amazing work. You have dedicated your lives to being a part of work you cannot finish. Keep going. It is hard. You don't hear thank you enough, but you must know future generations will live in a better world because of the impact of your efforts.

Rick Lopez, your talent never ceases to drop my jaw. I love seeing each chapter summarized and simplified through your illustrations. You are one of the best storytellers I know, and I am truly honored that you would contribute your God-given gifts to this book.

To Doug Robins, thank you for being a guide, a friend, and for recognizing that sometimes some of the most broken people hide way at the back of the church. To my sister, Gabriela Maestas O'dell, I love you. Thank you for always loving and supporting your baby brother. To my sisters, Christina Simek and Terrie Ulm, and brother, Mark Maestas. I adore you. Thanks for always loving your brother from another mother.

To my dad for teaching me to seek wisdom and for loving me even when it was not easy.

*Para mi mama* Lucinda de la Rosa. *Gracias por tu cariño y por tu apoyo. Tu eres el rason que todavia tengo mi negosio y por eso rason este libro y este trabajo esta dedicado a ti.*

To my wonderful mother-in-law, Patricia Rosas, and father-in-law, Robert Rosas. You welcomed Elijah and me into your family with open arms and have not let go since. Thank you to Ben and Jenny Rosas, Amy Rosas, and Mikey Rosas. Thank you for sharing your sister and nephew with me. I love being your family.

To Elijah, Jonathan, and Elyse. You represent the best part of my story. I feel so blessed to be your dad. Loving you and watching you grow into brilliant, beautiful people is worth every single grey hair you have given me. I pray that you will each live your best story.

To my favorite human, Jennifer Maestas. Thank you for being my best friend, my love, my partner, the rational half of my head and heart. Thank you for your unwavering belief in me. You embody why one should never give up when we think love might not be possible again. *Siempre serás mi amor profundo*. Google Translate that, lovey.

# About the Author

CARLOS MAESTAS believes storytelling is the best way organizations and people can move others to action. He is the founder and chief storysmith at Key Ideas, a Texas-based firm that helps organizations sharpen and share their messages. Carlos has interviewed thousands of people in his career, and since Key Ideas was started in 2002, it has won multiple awards and received five Lone Star EMMY nominations. A stand-up comedian who once opened for *Saturday Night Live* alum Dennis Miller, Carlos also has an MBA and leads a workshop called *Storytelling That Moves People* across the US. Carlos lives in San Antonio, Texas, with his wife and three kids.

# About the Illustrator

Rick Lopez is a San Antonio-based visual artist with a focus on storytelling through video production, animation, and illustration. He is currently a senior media producer within the H-E-B Grocery internal communications department. He enjoys creating videos about this amazing company while being both informative and entertaining.

He has an extensive background as an art director and a content creator. After a successful career working on national commercial campaigns and various local companies, he now applies his knowledge to help his production team create engaging videos that inform and inspire.

Rick is also known to create "sketchnotes" for conferences, corporate meetings, church gatherings, and design industry conferences. His illustrative note-taking skills help engage viewers and aid in understanding larger concepts.

When not working, he can be found: creating artistic illustrations, collaborating with his wife—musician Ruby Alexander, and raising two wonderfully creative young boys.

For more about Rick go to rick-o.com.

CPSIA information can be obtained
at www.ICGtesting.com
Printed in the USA
FSHW020631290620